EVOLVING THE ENTREPRENEUR

EVOLVE:

The progressive development and unfolding of the inner
INDIVIDUAL,
Triggered by specific internal or external *environmental shifts, For the purpose of psychological and physiological enhancement and advancement.

This shift is intended to expand the individual in a way that causes them to become more effective and more efficient at the purpose they've been called to fulfill. This shift is also intended to modify the individual in such a way that they become more suitable and more in influential throughout the territory in which they perform that purpose.

THE AUTHOR

A person's gift opens doors for them, bringing them access to important people.
- Proverbs 18:16

Hello, iAm DONOVAN.
iAm here to *change the way you think.*

I operate as a certified "Life Coach" in the greater Los Angeles area. From this vocation i share my gift with entrepreneurs who "put foot to pavement" everyday, fighting, thriving and strategizing to see the full manifestation of their hope and dreams. What you are going to experience this day, through the journey of this book ... is my "*gift*". For the entrepreneurs in this time and of this generation i come with this message...

"*Stop trying to experience Life and let Life experience you.*" –DonovanDeeDonnell

Everything i believe in is hinged on the truth that you are more than what meets the eye. **You are energy wrapped in flesh**. It is from this awareness and this truth that *i* began to evolve... and today i pray that i can help you to do the same.

This is my gift to my generation... enjoy.

INTRODUCTION :

Using a dull ax requires great strength, so sharpen the blade. That's the value of wisdom; it helps you succeed.
Ecclesiastes 10:10

What would you do if you felt like the things you *valued most were being threatened? Would you seek to simply survive the attack, or would you seek to **become the threat**. As an entrepreneur I've learned one very important thing: *no matter how good you are at defense , if you don't learn to play offense...you'll never win*. This book is not just about strategical self-defense. This book is about neutralizing the threat that opposes your goals and dreams **by becoming a threat to the enemy of your enterprise**. "Becoming the threat" is an aggressive approach but it's a very needed approach if you want to see true, lastings results. Most dictionaries have a very clear definition of what an "entrepreneur" is, but the essence of the entrepreneur is most deeply understood when you couple that definition with the understanding that "becoming the threat", very accurately describes what the entrepreneur has been called to do. But for an entrepreneur to adapt to that mindset, they must strategically approach the issue of *stagnation from the inside out*.

A strategic approach is designed to strike an enemy at the source of its power. This is why the strategical approach to stagnation must start with you, the entrepreneur, the one who is organizing and managing the enterprise. Why discuss the power and stance that stagnation has taken against your business, if we haven't first discovered how it acquired its position in your business in the first place. Stagnation has essential needs if it is going to exist. It needs a *foundation* to stand on and *fuel* to operate. If you are experiencing stagnation, understand that in one way or another, the foundation and fuel… *"were provided by you."* Stagnation usually acquires its power and position due to *mis-alignments* somewhere between entrepreneurial intentions and business mission/practices. It is vitally important that the entrepreneur identifies the mis-alignments in their business practices that are providing stagnation with the oxygen it needs to come against their entrepreneurial endeavors. Here is a question:

"In what area of your life, your business plan, your thought-process, your self-discipline, your emphasis on execution, *are you giving* stagnation the power to operate?"

These topics and many more, are a portion of what we will explore and dissect in this book. This book is designed to help you understand the most effective and efficient way to defeat stagnation and experience consistent profit. My approach starts with finding the root of the issue by exploring this very important question: Why did you come into the world of entrepreneurship in the first place? It is from *your exhausted response to this question that we will begin to "**deliver the first punch**" to the face of stagnation. Nothing unclogs the pipes better than introducing a substance that is stronger than the **object obstructing the flow**. What substance is strong enough to unclog the flow of your business profits... your "**why**". The *reason why you started is the foundation and strength on which you build momentum. Your "**why**" is the spine of your "enterprise body." If the reason you started is not **remembered and honored**, a stall and collapse are inevitable.

This book will not only deal with the general sense of entrepreneurship but will also provide probing questions and simple to use processes that will help you customize the insight given in this book to the specifics of your unique entrepreneurial life and the industry you have been called to. The field you have been called to can be a very volatile industry, so playing it safe is not an option if you want to affect true change or turn a profit. In essence, an entrepreneur runs toward risk, but hopefully not empty-handed **nor *empty-headed.** An entrepreneur abandons a certain level of safety for fulfillment of purpose. ***They enter the unknown...but they have a inner-knowing, a confidence and conviction that guides them to the helm of the industry they have been called to.*** A true entrepreneur has not come to duplicate but to innovate and that task comes with its challenges. The greatest of which are psychological. This book is designed to help you identify the true enemy, the true obstacles , the true purpose and the true possibilities. This is going to require us to do some internal work first, because just like a pregnant mother–the health and potential of the child is greatly dependent on the health of the vessel it passes through. You are that vessel and your business is that child. The more you evolve, the greater chance your child, or in this case, your business has at realizing its full potential and maximizing its existence in that industry.

Where there is no flow, there can be no growth, no impact, *no profit*. Where there is no flow, morale is low, the determination to exercise discipline diminishes and passion becomes frustration. But there is a solution and that solution lies within you, the entrepreneur… **you must, Evolve**.

AS YOU READ :

My son, pay attention to my wisdom, and listen closely to my insight so that you may act with *foresight and speak with insight
-Proverbs 5:1-2

Prepare yourself, a shift is about to take place. I pray that you take your time going through each chapter. Really chew on the words... i've intentionally chose them. To know me is to know that i thrive on clear effective communication. While going through this book, if their is a word that you aren't familiar with, you owe it to yourself and to your legacy to take the time to obtain clarity by looking up the definition. Don't allow any wealth to go un-attained, not one breakthrough to go unexperienced and no potential to go unrealized. This book is the opportunity you've been waiting for, ***this is your Evolution***. So, meditate on the ideas and the illustrations. They are intended to challenge "old beliefs"... that's what evolving is all about. Don't just try to read this book ...***experience it***. Go on the journey, truly consider the words next to the *asterisks, pausing for the ***words in italic*** and making note of the words in **bold print**. This book will bring new, exciting and valuable revelation no matter how many times you read it. This means you will never truly finish this book. Remember, iAM on this journey with you as well. May we ascend to new heights within ourselves, so that as we flow in our calling, we may experience the fullest manifestations of our true hearts desire and leave an invaluable legacy for all those who come behind us. In Jesus name, Amen !

> "Evolving the Entrepreneur is never a completed work, but an on-going process in which we must stay intentionally committed, or else our product or service will become ... obsolete." –DonovanDeeDonnell

CONTENTS

Entrust your work to the LORD, and your planning will succeed.
-Proverbs 16:3

•*consciousness*CHAPTERS

chapter 1:   AM I READY?..1
chapter 2:   WHY DOES THIS INDUSTRY NEED ME?..... 13
chapter 3:   HOSPITALITY IS THE KEY TO SUCCESS..... 19

•*commitment*CHAPTERS

chapter 4:   BOTH FEET IN............................. 27
chapter 5:   ESSENTIALS VS PURSUITS.................... 33
chapter 6:   BIRTH CONTROL 43
chapter7:   WHAT IS YOUR STRATEGY?.................. 51
chapter 8:   HOW IMPORTANT IS KNOWING
             YOUR NICHÉ?.................................61

•*care*CHAPTERS

chapter 9:   3 THINGS YOUR CLIENTS
             WANTS TO KNOW............................ 67
chapter 10: THE CUSTOMER IS ALWAYS RIGHT.......... 73
chapter 11: CELEBRATE OFTEN 81
chapter 12: REST AND MEDITATION..................... 87

ONE
AM I READY?

Am i ready?
Is the product ready?
Is the industry ready?

Are you ready to introduce *your* product or *your* service to *your* community? Are you ready to get the ball rolling, to start your business, to grow your business? Are you ready to go higher, to expand, to breakthrough to the next level? Many entrepreneurs have been trained to always say, "yes" to this question. But if your "yes" is based on desire alone, it has no depth, carries no weight and in essence, is meaningless. If you are truly ready, you should be able to ***prove it***. If you don't know how to identify if you are ready or how to prove that you are ready, this chapter is definitely for you. First, Let's blow this entrepreneurial myth out of the water:

- Saying you're ready doesn't actually "make you ready

There is more to truly being ready than just passion, ambition and confession. Wisdom tells us that, "*there is a correct time and place for all things to happen*" and "*everything is made beautiful it its own time.*" From this divine insight, the entrepreneur must understand that there is a right and wrong time in which to launch their business or implement a new strategy. And with that there is also a right and wrong area of the industry to "plant your presence". So, what does it really mean to be ready? To truly answer that question, we must start at the core.

At its core, ready, is "a state of being". Prepare is what *you do* and ready is what *you are*. Preparing is something that you are doing but *ready* is "when all essential elements are in *alignment*". In the business environment when asked , "are you ready" the person asking you is usually desiring to know 3 very specific things:

1. Are *you* prepared to organize and manage this business.
2. Is *your product* or service packaged for presentation and consumption.
3. How eager is "the industry" for what you plan to present.

Remember that "ready" is a state of being or the *condition* of a thing. The *condition* of something is based on 3 factors; *appearance*, *quality*, or *working order*. The *"state"* of something is determined by its *packaging*, its *integrity* and *functionality*. So, considering those three factors for *yourself*, your *product* and the *industry*... are you ready? Let's take some time to find out what ready *really looks like*, feels like, sounds like and how you can get there.

2

What i have put into place for my entrepreneurial clients is a system/process i call the "Abilities Quadrant".

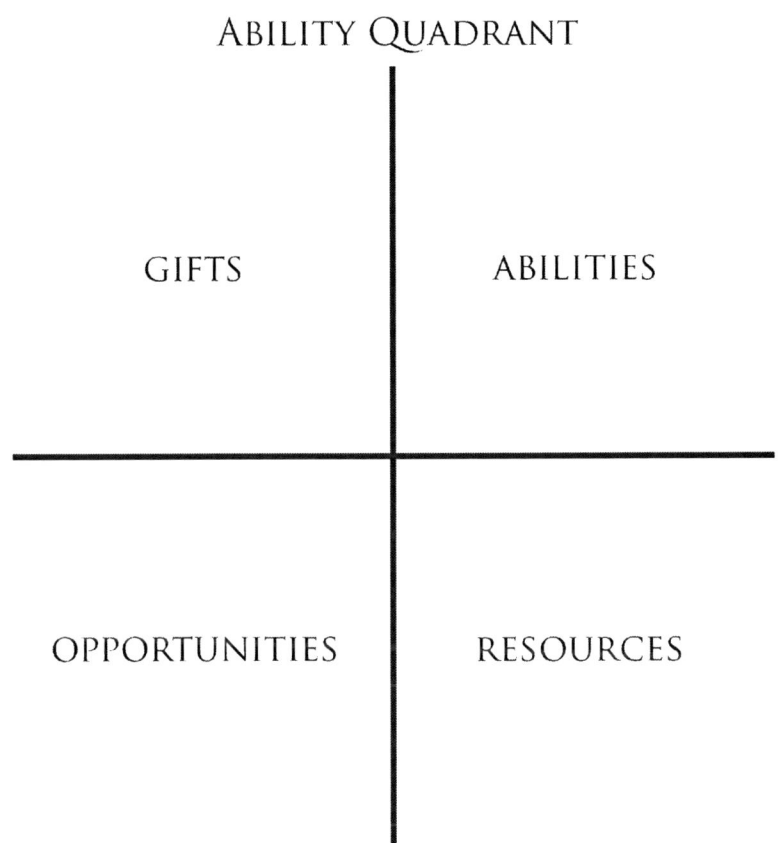

The first thing we do is explore the vision. What is the vision or goal that you have in your mind when it comes to this business you want to launch, the shift you want your business to experience or the impact you see yourself making on a specific industry. My clients and i spend a lot of time here talking about the details of the vision. Remember, we are not just trying to launch any business. We don't want to experience just any kind of shift. There are specific things that you want to manifest, specific shifts you want to experience, so really envision and *consider it all* through your 5 senses. What will it look like, smell like, sound like, taste like and feel like. This may seem silly, but the more details you have of your vision the more accurate your strategy can become. From here we look at their goal through 4 specific lens in hopes to answer that big questions, ***AM I READY to do*** this **specific thing*...and why?

- The 1st lens is their "internal *gifting*, authority or powers.
- The 2nd lens is their acquired *skills* from training or experience and exposure.
- The 3rd lens is their present and tangible *resources* or means.
- The 4th lens is any present *opportunities* or the evidence that the industry is presently in need of what you are offering.

This 4th lens focuses on timing and puts emphasis on the *advantage* a "properly timed birth" brings. These 4 lens are directly in-line with the definition of "able". Which is to have the power, skill, means or opportunity to do something. ***In many ways, "am i ready" is asking "am i able" to make the specific impact that i want to make or accomplish the mission I've been called to complete.*** This system helps to not only to bring us to the "yes or no" but also to the **why*. Proper execution of this system is contingent on the unique specifics of the participant and their endeavor. So if you intended to use this system on yourself or a client understand that the "expressed core values" ***of the entrepreneur*** is what allows the system to truly answer the question of am i ready and the why. In this chapter i will provide you with some of the same practical questions i present to my clients to help them gain two very important things.

1: gain more *clarity* and foresight :

which always results in more confidence and a more excellent level of operating.

2: gain more *awareness:*

which is intended to purify the motives, simplify the plan and enhance the level of peace, fulfillment and prosperity they have moving forward.

- Remember that the question "Am i ready" is to be applied not only to the entrepreneur but also the product/service and the industry.

GIFTING:

In the first lens we are considering the "***natural gifting***" or innate powers a person has. What innate abilities do you possess? This question begins to set the stage for the revelation or deeper revelation of their "created purpose". Knowledge of "created purpose" is key to every entrepreneur because if what you are pursuing isn't tied into your purpose in anyway , the pursuit will most likely not provide you with any true ***fulfillment*** , which for me is the ***foundational condition*** for success to be actualized. In the exploration of the entrepreneurs natural gifting we are finding not only their strengths but their **advantages**. A persons "natural gifting" are abilities given to them by God, pre-birth, that are specific to their purpose. The gifting gives each entrepreneur an advantage in a specific industry, for a specific time in order to complete a specific mission.

- "Could it be that you were born for such a time as this?

We can often find our passion or purpose in the specifics of our gifting, the innate abilities we have or the specific environment and unique set of circumstances in which we were born into."

Knowing your natural gifting provides great confidence and guidance which in turns helps with answering the question… "am i ready?"

ABILITIES:

In the second lens we explore the ***intentional personal development*** of the entrepreneur up to this present date. What experience, training and exposure have you had in the field, industry or arena in which you wish to make a impact with your service or product? Unlike the first lens, the second lens is not about innate abilities or gifts but it is a look into what the entrepreneur has done with their natural gifting so far. What tools, skills and awareness have you acquired that would help you to impact the industry "in the way that you desire"? While the first area of the quadrant focuses on what was given to you by God the divine, this area focuses on what you have given to yourself through, discipline, steps of faith, long-suffering, patience, resilience, sacrifice, planning and intentionality. This area of the quadrant looks at your present potential beyond the *"i was born to do this"* response and simply ask, ...*do you know how to do this*? This question is paramount to the entrepreneur because vision and passion alone is not enough. An entrepreneur is a "business person", who manages and organizes and enterprise, but their is no business if **Impact , Profit or Change** don't result from your effort. You can have the business cards, the business line and the business suit but if their is no strategy, business plan and no execution, is their really a business? So, the question "am i ready" is also a question of, what am i presently capable of doing? You are always ready ...to do something. But answering the question of, "am i ready to pursue and accomplish my ****specific goal***" will greatly depend on what you've done with your life, your gifts, your abilities and your time so far. Have you equipped yourself to make the impact you want to make on that industry?

RESOURCES:

In the third lens we look at "***resources***" which is the "***tangible means***." The can be anything from seed money, materials, staff or any other asset that you can presently draw upon in order to function effectively. What assets and relationships do you presently have in place that would help you to be successful in your pursuits in the industry that you desire to impact? The first lens of the quadrant is "***the divine***", what advantages were given to you prior to birth to ensure completion of your mission. The second lens is "*the self*", how have you equipped yourself up to this point in preparation of this pursuit. Now this third lens is "*the support*", the team or partners who will help you moving forward. This portion of the quadrant is not limited to just monetary and material assets but relational assets as in: mentors, investors, partners, potential employees or volunteers. *A *resource is a bridge between what's possible and what's actual.* A resource gives legs and life to your idea and is a major component in transforming your idea into a profitable business.

OPPORTUNITIES:

In the fourth lens we search for... the need... the "*industry demand*". We are opening our eyes and ears to recognize what it is that the consumer or industry is in need of. I do this by asking: "What opportunities or invitations have recently been extended to you for your service, product or input?" It is often that entrepreneurs attempt to flood a specific industry with a product or service that the consumer or industry hasn't expressed interest in... or need of. There is nothing wrong with this mode of action but if this is your plan, your **expectations must be properly managed* because you will "*first*" have the task of convincing the consumer they need this type of product, "before" you can build the momentum, see a profit, make an impact or cause the change. This fourth area of the quadrant is known as "*the season*", what are the present opportunities life is giving you to show you "it is time". Is this the most appropriate or most advantageous time to launch this endeavor ? Now, i will say this, "a farmer who waits for perfect weather conditions, never gets anything done." But that doesn't mean that the only factor to consider when desiring to get from point A to point B is the trajectory. It is in our best interest to consider the specific conditions and the unique set of circumstances that each ****season*** brings also. The quickest way may not alway be the safest way. The most clear path from point A to point B may be a straight line ... but it is wise to look both ways before you cross the street. With consideration of my gifts, the present development of my skills and the reliability of my resources , is this the most advantageous time to launch? The entrepreneur should answer this question ****heavily considering*** the outcome they desire. This portion of the quadrant can be lost in translation so it is important to remember that the time you launch is predominantly based on the "outcome you desire to see". It may not be the most advantageous for monetary profit , but if monetary profit is not the main focus then this may actually be the most advantageous time to launch. This area of the quadrant truly helps the entrepreneur to gain a better perspective of the present need for the product or service they desire to supply. That ***enhancement*** of perspective will help to identify the most advantageous time and area of the industry to launch their endeavor in.

THE ANSWER:

Now that all four quadrants are completed, refer back to the "detailed vision" you created in the beginning. Based on the information inside the gifts, skills, resources and opportunities quadrants... are you ready? Do you possess the needed gifts, skills or resources to launch that *specific* business or create "that specific" enterprise shift... right now? Are there presently any opportunities being presented to you to do "that specific thing"? It is in considering your entrepreneurial desires through the lens of the abilities quadrant that you begin to see if *all the essentials elements are in alignment* for a launch to take place. if they are not, it doesn't mean you can't move forward. It simply means that you are not ready to do "that specific thing". At this stage you are now also able to see what's missing. It is in the completion of the abilities quadrant that my clients truly see if they are ready *and why*. When my clients can honestly say, "yes i am ready" after completing the quadrant, it is because they can look at each quadrant and see "*why*" they are ready and that brings a great sense of confidence. When my clients say, "no they are not ready", they can also look at the quadrant and see *exactly where* the lack is. This is extremely beneficial because they don't waste time trouble-shooting every area of their business plan or strategy. They can see with clarity if a skill or resource is needed or if the timing isn't right. They can also see if they don't have the necessary gifts for that specific vision. When it comes to "lack in the gifts quadrant", i advise my clients to take a moment to pray and seek divine clarity. Sometimes my clients aren't aware of all their gifting and they need to seek God, the giver of the gifts, and search deeper within themselves. Then there are sometimes when the entrepreneur is simply pursuing an industry or mission that simply isn't for them. Just because you are passionate about something, doesn't make it your purpose. This is the benefit and power of the abilities quadrant. You don't just gain an answer to the question, you also can uncover the why.

The ability quadrant is a great tool to *gain perspective*. "How" the entrepreneur views themselves and interprets the industry will determine how successful they will be. Enhancing the entrepreneurs ability "***to see***", in turn enhances their ability to do everything else. With what i shared with you in this chapter you can begin that "perspective shift journey" and truly gain a clearer answer to the questions of "Am i ready?" and "why". The quadrant and the questions asked above are all geared to help the entrepreneur see into the readiness of themselves, the product/service and the industry in which they will provide their product or service. Again, it is "evidence of ***alignment***" or "areas of needed re-aligning" and development that we are searching for in the abilities quadrant.

TWO
WHY DOES THIS INDUSTRY NEED ME?

What are the **intentions** that drive your ambition?

Ambition is the key ingredient that enables the entrepreneur to take *immediate and calculated advantage* of the opportunities that come their way. But in all honesty, *if the intention behind their ambition is not in line with their mission,* even the most ambitious entrepreneur can "lose their way", ruin the reputation of their business and become stagnant. If fulfillment and success are your desire, your determination to succeed should never be in moral conflict with the "*foundational principles*" and moral reason why you became an entrepreneur in the first place.

- "To succeed but not be able to sleep at night is not success."

One of the benefits of purifying your motives and "aligning your principles and practices" is the ***advantage and influence*** you gain overtime in that industry. This means that it will require much patience, self-confidence and discipline. But when "advantage and influence" are obtained, it is then that you truly possess the power to make a lasting impact. This is what enables an entrepreneur to fulfill their mission and accomplish their calling, which was their foundational reason for organizing, existing and birthing the business in the first place. I'll be honest, keeping your standard and not compromising your morals can be difficult at times because of the tempting allure of the spotlight, the lust for power, the dread of embarrassment and the need to turn a profit due to business cost and expenses. But the most unfortunate disadvantage that arises when morals are compromised and business "principles and practices" are not in alignment is, ***entrepreneurial sabotage**". This means that your business loses all eligibility to potentially gain any real influence in that industry. This also means that your business loses all ability to become a tool for positive change in that industry. And most of all this means that the maximum profit you are ***allowed*** to turn will always be determined by *_the people you sold your soul to_. So, who is ready to purify their motives and align their principles and practices?

Creating "*practical purification practices*", for yourself or your team, is one way to keep your entrepreneurial motives in alignment. This can be very fun and very rewarding if it is done right, so be creative and intentional. I will give you a popular example, but always make sure that your purification practices are specifically customized to address your specific mission and tailored to the personalities of all those under your employ. Some companies like to have every employee carry around a business card with the mission statement on it and have set times in which they read the mission statement aloud to themselves. As simple as it sounds, when done consistently, it has proven to be very effective at keeping the entrepreneur "true to who the say they are." The purification practice that is put in place should flow well with the culture of the business, the energy of the office and reflect the heart of the founder because the main point is to keep the "*why*" prioritized. In doing this the entrepreneur is better able to maintain the standard by intentionally honoring the core values of their enterprise.

- It is in the **remembrance* of the "why" that the "why" stays strong.

Another purification practice i've seen a few times, is a business taking time daily to meditate and *chant the mission statement of their business. This is a very good business practice if you and your employees value a good chant every now and then, but if not, find one that works for you. Meditating is a high value of mine so this practice is one i've put into place to ensure that every daily decision i make stems from the foundational values that i set in place when the vision and business were first birthed in my heart. I've had many conversations with seasoned and seemingly successful business people where i was encouraged to simply "*play the game*". They told me, sometimes "*dirty play*" is necessary if you want to remain relevant and experience monetary success. Fortunately my grandfather was a very successful business man and i had the privilege to glean from his business mind and practices. One of the main things he put forth much effort to teach me was the importance of **reputation**. Your name needs to mean something and with every business decision you make–you are deciding what your name will mean when spoken in the business and consumer world. Also, my grandmother was the motivation behind the name of my photography company; "donbg photo". The "donbg" was a name but also a shortened version of the phrase, "donnie be good". This was one of the moral pillars of my photography business. The reminder was "***to do good business even if everyone else around you wasn't,*** because being honest and fair is a great *seed to plant* if you want to continue experiencing **true prosperity.**

How you "*do*" business will determine how you will be remembered in the business that you've done. Dirty play may bring temporary satisfaction or monetary gain, but in the long run, how will it affect your reputation? If you are not a part of the solution in that industry, you are the problem. Take a moment to remember your reason for existence in the industry that you are in and ask yourself, are you bringing the solution, relief and innovation that you have been called to bring, or has self-glorification and personal gain become the aim of your efforts? What i want you to see in this chapter is that the idea of purifying your motives resonates very deeply with the business person that is **legacy minded*. There are many "burn-out businesses" that never desired longevity but *if* your desire is to one day pass this business on to a family member or dear friend, consider what assets, liabilities, and reputation you want attached to the business once it transitions into their care.

Becoming legacy minded is one of the premier perspective shifts an entrepreneur can make in combating stagnation , moral compromise and entrepreneurial sabotage. Taking serious time to sit down and consider *why* your business exist, *what* type of long term impact you want to make on the industry and *where* you see this business going once you are gone–truly begins to navigate you down a unique and highly profitable professional path that many miss because of their lust for the spotlight or immediate gratification.

- When you lust after the spotlight, you run the risk of perverting your gift. "The spotlight comes with a high cost when it is pursued, but when it finds you on its own, it only yields the ***fruit of success*** which is fulfillment, prosperity and influence."

So when you are asked, what is your reason for existence, my hope is that you answer through the lens of your desired legacy. To give you another personal example of my approach to answering "my reason for existence", i will share with you a daily prayer that sums up my desires as a business man.

"Father God, enlarge my territory *so that i may* more perfectly honor you with my gift. Father God, partner with me *so that i may* properly steward this blessing and father God, lead me not into temptation *so that i will not* mess it up.

My approach to business, even if i am the owner, founder or CEO, is to operate as a ***steward*** because in my mind the business idea was given to me but the business belong to and has been dedicated to God. God gave me the idea, the gifting and the position of a steward so that i would combine them all in such an excellent way that a specific service or product is provided to those in need and that God is Glorified in "*how*" it is done.

THREE
HOSPITALITY IS THE KEY TO SUCCESS

Without the client…where would you be?

"No matter what industry i am in… i am in the *Hospitality Business*." At the core of every plan, every practice, every strategic move, the entrepreneur should be considering this very important question, "How will this business practice affect the client?" If you want your customers or clients to be loyal, the entrepreneur must see them as more than a consumer. If every person you interacted with in a professional setting was treated like an honored guest in a five star hotel… what do you think customer loyalty and your client referrals would look like? There is a residue that remains after every interaction we have with another person. Call it energy, vibe or a feeling… there is an impression that remains. This impression, this feeling, that vibe, is the foundational force that will draw them back to you or drive them away. When the entrepreneur becomes aware of the "power of residue", they then see the value of being intentional, professional and present whenever they are publicly representing their company. The beautiful part is, it's very easy to make someone feel "cared for" and it cost the entrepreneur absolutely nothing to be kind, attentive and respectful. Let's dive deeper into what hospitality really looks like.

Is your goal to get the product sold or to *also enhance* the life of those who buy it or buy into it? These kind of questions help make you aware of how aligned or mis-aligned your intentions are with the **true foundational mission of** *entrepreneurship* The *condition* of that alignment greatly influences how successful you can be. So, you've created something that you believe someone is in need of. Don't just focus on the "something", focus on the "someone". Wether your desire is to turn a profit, make an impact or influence change, this will only come to pass when you place appropriate focus on *who* you are providing your service or product to. An entrepreneur does this primarily by focusing on "***the quality***" of that product or service we provide because what better way to show you truly care about the "consumer" than to provide them with ***the best you can offer.*** You will also need to set much of your attention on "*how*" you provide that product or service because h*ow* you do "that something" is a direct reflection of w*hy* you "do that something and making known your why is where you have the greatest potential, to gain your clients trust. Trust is paramount.

We are often taught that the stagnation or decline of a business is usually a direct result of ; ***poor management , insufficient capital, location, lack of planning, over expansion or poor promotion.*** But the biggest error or enemy of any business' growth will always be found in the

business practices that directly affect the overall personal well-being of the client or customer in a negative way. The trust of the customer, client, consumer... is the blood line of your business. Without it, the business will whither and die. Many businesses fail because their present focus has drifted away from the "initial reason for existence." This happens often and that is why i want to address this issue in this chapter. The entrepreneur must stay true to their "***initial why***" if they are to see the goal accomplished. You don't want to be the entrepreneur who says one thing in public but operates in a totally different spirit behind closed doors. This kind of behavior eats away at the potential life expectancy of your business simply because, "what happens in the dark, always comes to the light." When the mission statement and the business practices are out of alignment with "true entrepreneurship", the business will experience "foundational challenges" which, if not corrected, will cause the business to collapse within itself. Manipulation is not sustainable, which means that manipulative behavior, if continued, will be the catalyst for the collapse of your enterprise.

- A kingdom divided against itself cannot stand.- Mark 3:24

Do you care "*for*" your clients... or, do you only care "*about*" your clients? Caring ***about*** the client is different from caring ***for*** the client. Caring ***for them*** goes beyond only considering how they can help you or your business. I believe that many entrepreneurs come into their industry with a clear mind, pure heart and desire to care for their clients... but if the entrepreneur doesn't understand how great of an impact "caring for" the client can make, determination to do so will fade away underneath the daily "operational weight" of the business. I also believe, the global consciousness of this present generation has birthed many entrepreneurs who deeply desire to care for the client, but don't really have a practical effective approach of "how to." I will speak greatly to that issue in the chapter entitled, "3 things your client wants to know."

I know this is not every entrepreneurs desire, but let me say this, If it's all for the money, i want you to be aware of where **that road ends** and where compromise of your morals and values must begin. My personal belief is:

- *in order to keep continual success as a part of my yearly reports, the motives behind my professional existence must be rooted in holding *hospitality as the premiere thing. Valuing hospitality above everything else and choosing to build my business on the fact that it is a privilege and honor to serve a community of people with my gifts, talents and abilities.*

The atmosphere this approach to entrepreneurship creates will always attract the *type of people* you desire to service. Does this mean that sales will always be sky high, maybe , maybe not, but there will always be a flow. Now, i understand that it takes real money to run a business. But i also understand that you can chase money or attract it. Some people forget that chasing money is not the only option. I understand that competitors exist and will do inhumane things to sabotage your business, but success will not be obtained if we waste energy repaying evil for evil, that energy can be better invested toward the goal. Energy spent is either energy invested… or it is energy wasted when it's not driving you closer to accomplishing your mission in a way that doesn't compromise your morals and principles. I know the temptations to compromise your morals will arise so that bills can be paid and so that doors can remain open. I've had to face that giant many times, but in those times i remember two things, my legacy and the 3 promises i've made to myself. I encourage all my clients to make 3 promises to themselves concerning their business. This is their "*personal law*".

1. i promise to always …
2. i promise to never …
3. i promise to remember …

These 3 promises are intended to remind the entrepreneur of the value of there "*why*". There are many trials that will await the entrepreneur and the temptation to compromise has always been one that is dear to my heart because

- *if we, as entrepreneurs drink the poison, we then begin to serve the poison to the people we say that we are honored to serve.*

We also pervert the gift that we were given prior to birth which is a slap in the face of our creator. The spirit of *hospitality* is rooted in generosity and prioritizing the needs of the customer/client, over the need for profit. Hospitality is rooted in the awareness that "the people" are to be loved and things are to be used, not the other way around. When things are in order ... things fall into place. When the main thing, ***hospitality, is acknowledged and prioritized*** as the main thing– resources, profit, prosperity, influence and everything else will flow in abundance. Flow...that is the opposite of stagnation. Could it be that we keep missing the "shot of profit" because we are only focused on making the profit instead of focusing on what causes the profit to be made?

I recall learning to play basketball. All i wanted was to put the ball in the hole. My coach knew this and started teaching me "correct form" and body mechanics. At first i didn't get it. I knew how to bend my knees and push the ball and flick my wrist. I mimicked what i saw others do, but i didn't really understand "how they did it". What i didn't understand was the importance of those specific things happening in a specific order and within a specific structure. So, i practiced and practiced and my coach continued to watch me shoot. Strangely enough, he knew when i was focused on making the shot and when i was focused on my form. He could call the shot as a make or miss before it even left my hands. I was so frustrated with how he knew if i would make the shot or not. But one day while playing alone, i became so frustrated ... i gave up trying to make the shot. I took a deep breath, found my spot and planted my feet. I bounced the ball twice, bent my knees a few times, slowly raised the ball from my waist, to slightly in front of my face and thought about every sequential movement my coach had told me, and

…. BOOM! I made the shot. I was happy, but i figured it was just a game of numbers and eventually i was destined to make the shot. So, i tried the process again, and …BOOM, another goal. I repeated this specific process and every time i did it in the right sequence i made the shot. This blew my mind. When i stopped focusing on making the shot and simply focused on *what was required* in order for a shot to be made, my shot improved dramatically.

This story is just to add emphasis on the importance of focusing on the structure, the strategy, the foundational principles, prioritizing the important things and trusting that the desired flow of my business will result from the *corrected flow* within my business practices. Customer service and hospitality are essentials in business and should be given the appropriate attention and energy if success is to be realized. It may seem odd to not focus on the profit, but if you have been called to a specific industry and gifted to make an impact, have faith that your divine advantage was always intended to produce a profit but it is always dependent on how focused you are on the *core of "what you been called to do."*

- "No matter what industry i am in, no matter what product or service i provide , i am in the *Hospitality Business*."

FOUR

BOTH *FEET* IN

Is this where i belong?
Can i handle this load?
Will it be worth it?

Taking on the mantle of an "entrepreneur" can be exciting and at the same time terrifying. So as you leave the *employee mindset,* here are a few things you will want to make sure you have packed in your bag. Courage, confidence and curiosity. Each of these are vitally important to maximizing and realizing the potential of your business: courage is a specific lens in which you **examine** *yourself,* confidence is a specific lens at which you **analyze** *the process* or the journey and curiosity is a specific lens through which you **envision the** *possibilities*. How you see yourself, how you see the process and how you see the possibilities is what separates those who succeed from those who don't, because "how you see" determines *what you do. It also separates those who succeed without compromising there morals, from those you lose their souls in the process.

So which of these three do you think is the most important when it comes to starting your business, growing your business or accomplishing your mission? How you see yourself, how you see the process or how you see the possibilities? Let's see. **Confidence** focuses on what "you" are up against or "in for". **Curiosity** in this sense, is all about the creative, what could this become in a future time. **Courage** determines if we will move forward and how far forward we will move. So which holds the most weight and carries the greatest influence on the success of your business? They are one, like the car, the key and the driver. All three are required to get you moving from here to another place called there. Courage, confidence and curiosity all play a specific role and if one isn't present, the launch will be hindered or compromised. My ability to launch forward in the face of uncomfortability and unfamiliarity is limited or strengthened by my belief of: *do i feel i've been built for this* (courage). My ability to launch forward is also limited or strengthen by my view of the process, which is; what i believe will be required of me and if i believe i can handle all of it (confidence). What will drive me to launch or procrastinate, is if i can *see an outcome that i feel ***justifies the requirements of the process***(curiosity).

Is this where i belong? Can i handle this load? Will it be worth it? These questions are a family, they lean on one another and when they are in alignment something great happens... people *commit*. When your answer to; is this where i belong, can i handle this load and will it be worth it, is *a un-compromised, soul stirring yes*–you don't just bind yourself to that endeavor, you're recognizing that it has always been a part of who you are. At the exact moment of my consciousness, there also was my calling …and this is it. That is the essence of true commitment.

When you can honestly answer yes to these three questions, the awakening you experience allows "true commitment" to take place. It is in this awareness that you realize that you can't escape the mission, avoid this call or replace this passion. When true commitment takes place, it is not an act of trying to attach yourself to something or someone.

- *Commitment is the act of addressing your issues, correcting your behavior and fine tuning your focus so that what has always been a part of you, attached to you, made for you–may come forth… like it was always intended to do.*

This definition of commitment reveals that it is impossible to commit to something you haven't been divinely called to. And how can you experience fulfillment if their is no commitment?

So, how does a person get to that place of commitment? Consider the vision you have for your business. How would that vision be enhanced if you had both feet in? (*pause*) Maybe you responded , "…i have both feet in". My question to you then is this. How would the vision of your business be enhanced if you ventured off into the deep? (*pause*) Both feet in is just the beginning. If you are experiencing stagnation, my first question is, "are you all in", have you answered yes to the three questions? Life has a way of recognizing and responding to our *timidity. If we are not all in, if we don't have both feet in, it shows in how we behave and that behavior is telling "life" that we are *unsure. And being unsure results from lack of courage, confidence and/or curiosity. Are you sure about this career, this field, this plan, this calling, this timing? If you are not, it will show in your hesitation and procrastination and you will subconsciously always be "**holding back**"... *and since life let's us lead the dance*, it will politely do the same. Remember my philosophy on life, "*Stop trying to experience life and let life experience you*." I am a firm believer that Life is subject to our actions, reaction and responses. Life follows our lead. We are not waiting for life to happen, life is constantly responding to what we cause to happen. So consider your business stance, your business posture ...are you all in? Consider your meditations, declarations and conversations... is this your destiny? Do you really believe in the success of this idea, do you believe in the impact it will make on the industry you have been called to?

If you truly believe in it and can see the success of it, i am going to help you lay a foundation to launch from. Remember that the "call" is evidence that you will succeed. As you stay on the path, being driven by the vision and directed by your core values, you will have the fulfillment of seeing the mission accomplished and your family and friends enjoying the abundance from the seeds you have sown. Below are seven categories for a solid foundation.

1–MISSION (why we exist / purpose)

11–VISION (where we are going)

111–CORE VALUES (morals and non-negotiables)

1V–GOALS (milestones / pre-set achievements)

V–STRATEGY (the detailed road map)

V1–TACTICS (the field decision that drive the strategy)

V11–VITAL BEHAVIOR (the required conduct based on the vision)

So what is it going to take to get you launched or unstuck and running smoothly…? Fill in your answers for each of the categories listed above. From there you expand and get as detailed as possible for each one. To complete this portion you will have to look at your business, your calling and your passion through each of the lens mentioned in this chapter.

How you view yourself, the process and the possibilities all begins with the layout, the structure, the wide view. As you meditate and consider the future possibilities–what you are doing is creatively considering multiple strategy options that will lead to your success, and **if you can envision yourself succeeding**–you have obtained the most valuable asset to your success. It all starts with envisioning the "Win". But that is difficult to do until we have a clearer picture of "what we are up against, what we are made of and what all that could possibly mean for our legacy. Hear me when i say this, "*you are perfectly made for what you've been called to do*". I've spent intentional time preparing the first few chapters to help you identify your "true calling". By now you have much more clarity and with that clarity i say again, you are perfectly made for what you've been "*called*" to do. You have been divinely equipped to accomplish the mission that you have been created and selected for. You have been divinely built for this. This business you are launching into existence or to another level will be launched or limited only by your faith and your faith is subject to your confidence, your courage and your curiosity. Step in and go deep. Only look back to appreciate how far you have come. This is where you belong, you are built for this, you can handle this and yes, yes it will be worth it. Because this is a part of who you are, you will not only pursue it, it will pursue you. As committed as you are to it, remember that it is also committed to you. When you commit, understand that you are now driving toward and simultaneously being drawn to your destiny.

FIVE
ESSENTIALS VS PURSUITS

What do entrepreneurs eat for breakfast?

"For what does it profit a man, to gain the world, but lose his soul." This is a phrase that often comes to mind in the entrepreneurial coaching world. How do you strive for what's next, without neglecting what's now? How can i *obtain* more… and still *maintain* what's already in my possession? If i stop pursuing, does that mean I'm settling? Today, i want to let you know that there is a way to have it all. A good friend of mine would often tell me, "Donovan, don't let the things you want make you forget the things you have." I didn't know why, but this phrase always had a way of bringing, what felt like *balance, back to my life. One day i decided to take a deeper look into this phrase and i asked myself, how could what i want… make me forget what i have?

I realized that most entrepreneurs, truly throw themselves into their endeavors. They are, "all-in", as we discussed in the previous chapter. When a new idea comes; they gather all their gifts and skills and resources, they settle into their own "creative cubicle" and they start the process.

This usually happens in isolation but sometimes within a small team of people. But... what about everything else... everyone else, that existed prior to your pursuit of this new endeavor? What happens to all that? This is how marriages fail, friends become strangers and the quality of a persons health declines. Many entrepreneurs would like to believe that they can press the "***auto-pilot***" button and the marriage, friendships and their health will take care of themselves while they pursue their endeavor. But something about that doesn't seem quite right. How can something so important, so valuable to you, become so secondary because of this new idea you've been ***called*** to pursue? Some people believe that, this is simply the price you pay to succeed as a entrepreneur. Today i want you to understand that the price has already been paid.

- ***Remember, your gift is evidence that if you move by faith, you will succeed. You have been divinely called to this work, this mission, this industry.***

You don't have the pay the "outsiders fee", there is no blood sacrifice required for your entrance to ***this work***. You have been called here, there is already a spot reserved for you. There is no initiation, no one to prove yourself to. There is simply a place in which you are to serve your gift to those in need. So, "never let what you want make you forget what you have". Contrary to what i initially thought, this phrase didn't bring me balance, it brought *****awareness***. Awareness of the value of what i presently have. It helped to remind me of this simple, but significant truth:

"what i *already have*, is what allows, equips, empowers and frees me me to go after what i want" In this sense of *having, I'm speaking of; my healthy relationships, my peace of mind, the ability and fluidity of my limbs and organs. These *essential* things dictate how effective of an entrepreneur i will be.

Understanding that these things are essential: ***absolutely necessary*** to the core health, wellness and effectiveness of who i am as a man and as a entrepreneur, i became aware and i recognize that ****no-gain could compare to the lost of an essential***, *because… no gain could truly be obtained if i lost or neglected an essential.* Again, the value set on the essentials should be based on this understanding; the essentials allow, equip, empower and free the entrepreneur to pursue and accomplish the endeavor. So, if the essentials are not maintained, the endeavor will not be obtained. I say this because i learned a very important lesson at a business leadership conference i attended. The main speaker reminded all the entrepreneurs in the room that, "the difference between an idea and a business is the *profit." It is not a business until it yields some sort of profit. Throughout this book you will see me refer to "profit" as a monetary profit, or gaining influence in a industry or causing your desired shift on the market. I explain this to help us understand that there are many "types of profits" that can be made but only one way to calculate true profit. Let's say you accomplish the endeavor you pursued, at the *expense of your essentials. What is your profit, if profit is : *the gain* identified by the difference?

Yes you may have earned a large sum of money in the completion of this endeavor...

- ***but before we can determine the profit, we must *deduct the value of the *essentials that you lost or neglected during the pursuit of the endeavor.***

Essential number one, if you neglected your health in pursuit of your endeavor and your health failed or you acquired health issues that required medication, how would you calculate "that expense" in dollars and cents? How much will it cost to repair your health to where it was prior to you pursuing the endeavor? Essential number two, what about your marriage and the other healthy relationships that helped you become who you were? How much will it cost to repair those connections and re-build those bridges of trust, reliability and access? What does it profit a man to gain the world, but lose his soul? This verse from the bible is what the foundation of this chapter is rooted in. It is here that i want to discuss *"essentials vs. pursuits"*.

ESSENTIALS:

So let's just say, the essentials mentioned above are not your essentials. Have you identified what your essentials are? What is absolutely necessary for you as a person and as a entrepreneur? What kind of environment must you be in to maximize your potential? Maximizing your potential is like when you buy milk from the store. You can bring it home and put it in the fridge, or leave it on the counter for easier access. But *where you place it determines how long it will last.

- The ideal environment allows the true potential to be realized.

If my environment has the influence to determine how long i will last and how much of my potential can be realized, i now recognize having a specific environment as an essential because of it's ability to prolong my life and enhance my effectiveness. With this understanding i take extra special care to create a specific kind of environment around me through the relationships i intentionally tend to, the hobbies i involve myself in and the thoughts i allow myself to meditate on. All of these areas must be attended to if i am to create and maintain an environment that will best maximize my potential. So again, what kind of environment must you be in, what relationships or elements must be present in your day to day life in order to maximize your potential, in order to extend your life, and enhance your effectiveness as an entrepreneur?

I mentioned above about how the quote my friend said to me, caused me to feel a sense of balance, but to my surprise it wasn't balance, it was *awareness* that i felt. This is where i came to understand that in life and in business, balance is only part of what *allows the flow* to continue. "*You balance your pursuits, but you prioritize your essentials*". The essentials are what allow you to be the caliber of entrepreneur you truly want to be. So why give pursuits and essentials equal or balanced attention and energy, when the essentials are the foundational elements of your life that will ultimately fuel you to accomplish the pursuit without compromising your morals? No one person is successful in and of themselves. In one way or another, there are always other elements at play or relationships they have partnered with to obtain their success. For instance: if my marriage is getting what it needs, my wife becomes a partner, my home becomes a refuge and that effects greatly how well i perform as a entrepreneur. If i don't get enough rest or enough water, it won't take long before my performance suffers and my ambition begins to lose momentum because water is an *essential to life.

Why is the idea of essentials vs. pursuits so vital for the entrepreneur? Let's look at the basic idea of what an entrepreneur is.

An entrepreneur is one who organizes and manages a business or an enterprise. With this basic definition, we can safely say that, an entrepreneurs success will be determined by how well they "organize and manage". Well... what would help a person to be more organized? Personally, i'd say a clear and organized mind. What would give or allow a person to have a more organized mind? Things like, good sleep, healthy meals and *confidence that their "valuables" are safe*. Those are a few things that help *me* to have a more organized mind and operate in my flow as a entrepreneur. These things are also on my list of "essentials". The reason is, without them i can't really call myself an entrepreneur, because without them, my *ability* to organize and operates fails tremendously. Hopefully now you are beginning to see that the good sleep, quality food and confidence that my valuables are safe, are the things that ***allow*** me, equip me, empower me and "free me" to organize and operate my business with passion, high quality effectiveness and efficiency. When i don't get these essentials it is very evident in *how* i organize and operate. And when my "organization and operation are failing", my business has no choice but to do the same. So, what is the essential and what is the pursuit? In this case, the essential, the things that are absolutely necessary, is the good sleep, quality food and confidence that my valuables are safe. The pursuit is the success of my business. The understanding here is; **without the essentials, accomplishing the pursuit is impossible.* If the essentials are ignored, neglected or compromised–you won't have what you need to realize a real profit.

- *"The essentials are the foundation on which fulfillment and success will manifest".*

I have a question and a exercise for you: *"What makes it easier for you to go into work, be peaceful and productive, turn a profit and make an positive impact on the industry that you are in?"* After truly considering this question, taking a sheet of paper, making two categories and marking one side, essentials and the other pursuits and filling it in, will be one of the most beneficial exercises you could complete once you've finished reading this chapter.

- *Remember, people don't always plan to compromise, they simply fail to identify their *non-negotiables.*

Did you know that water performs such a unique and important function in the body, that without an adequate supply, the body will shut down? There is no substitute for it and it affects everything. Understanding this is what helps you recognize water as an essential, a non-negotiable, absolutely necessary ingredient to your success. When the essentials are prioritized it doesn't matter how many pursuits you have on your list, they can all be accomplished in their season. This way of thinking was made clear to me by my grandfather. He told me, "start with the top button and all the other buttons will fall into place". My hope is that you identify the main thing (essentials) and that you keep the main thing the main thing and that you maintain the main thing so that your God given purpose may be realized in every season of you life. What does it profit a man to gain the world but lose his soul? I read that question this way; what did you "*really *gain*" from obtaining all the possessions you wanted ...after we **deduct the value of your soul**, since it was lost in the process. The soul is known to many as "the mind". So i re-ask the question. What does it profit a person to gain material possessions but lose his mind in the process?

In conclusion my prayer is that you are given clarity as to the value of the essential things that have purposely been placed in your life. That there is *no further neglect of the people you have been called to partner* with and the *health you have been called to maintain*. My prayer is that "peace of mind" is seen as a premiere asset and that you remember that you can do all things through Christ who gives you strength. When the essentials are prioritized over the pursuits, the entrepreneur increases their defense against lost or stagnation. This is because the source from which success will flow is being given the top priority. And when the health of the foundation is *that strong and every business decision is required to **first answer to the core values** ...success and flow are inevitable. Even with the present knowledge of the immense value of the essentials, when the entrepreneur enters their flow, the value of the essentials are easily forgotten. This is why we must write them down and place them somewhere as a constant daily reminder. We know how important they are but often the entrepreneur struggles with "urgent vs. important." I encourage my entrepreneurs to put their essentials list in 3 places. Home, vehicle, work, screen saver. Somewhere that it will capture you for a moment and the essentiality of the essentials can set into your spirit once again. Often, it is the practical... that truly helps us achieve the super natural.

SIX

BIRTH *CONTROL*

At what point does my *increase* cause my *downfall*?

A very common question to ask someone who is preparing to be married is, "how many children do you want?" That question has always seemed difficult to me. It seems like another very important element is missing from the question that would really help me to have a more truer and accurate response. Something like: "How many children do you want and how far apart to do you want the children to be born?" This allows for a more detailed picture to form in my mind of the **realities** and **responsibilities** of birthing these new bundles of joy. What is my capacity and what is the capacity of my partner and i? How many children can we: this household, this family, handle *at once* and not be overwhelmed or *forced to neglect other essentials*? This is where we find the importance of having the "*frequency*" conversation, which is the rate at which something occurs or is repeated over a particular amount of time.

In America, many birth control options deal with that specific element ..."frequency". Some people, immediately after the wedding, want to get straight to the baby making / baby birthing part of the marriage and hopefully have 3 or 4 children within the first 4-5years. Other people want to spread the children out 3 or 4 years in between each one. Who is to say which is the better choice? It is not a conversation of right or wrong but rather a conversation on *capacity* that every engaged and newly wed couple needs to have. What can you handle without losing personal quality of life, damaging the relationship between you and your spouse or ***diminishing* "the quality of rearing"** that each child is raised in. In simple terms, consider the responsibility that comes with the beautiful opportunity of being a parent.

- *When there is an opportunity, there is always a responsibility and where there is a responsibility, there needs to be a strategy.*

When it comes to the rate at which you and your partner birth a child into this world, you both should be as intentional as possible. This is why i encourage my engaged or married clients to map out, in detail, the vision for their marriage. The more detailed their vision, the more aware they will become of the "***best times*** to give birth". Of course there are always unexpected situations that arise, but our responsibility is to do the best with what we are aware of. There is no limit to how prepared you can try to make yourself. Sitting down with your partner and a coach or mentor to intentionally ***make yourself as aware*** as possible about the shifts and responsibilities of birthing a child into this world, greatly increases your chances of preventing stagnation, frustration, divorce and abortion.

I believe this same approach is beneficial for entrepreneurs. If you are reading this book, you are… or you know, a entrepreneur that has multiple business ideas, let's call that–children they want to give brith to. And in many cases the business ideas are in no way related to one another–we can call that *multiple mothers.* In many of my conversations with entrepreneurs, most have 3 or 4 great business ideas that they are equally as passionate about. But as a mentioned before,

- *"intentions are great but **capacity is king**".*

The initial question that i present every entrepreneur with that has multiple business ideas is … "*at what point will your quality of life, quality of production or quality of service begin to suffer*?" Do you know your capacity? This is an important question because i truly hate to see an entrepreneur who is full of passion become full of frustration as a result of having too much on their plate. Let it be known, it doesn't make you a better parent if you have 3 children back to back to back or if you wait 3 years in between each child. Likewise for the entrepreneur, if the main goal of the businesses is to bring profit, impact or cause change, it is in our best interest to begin to properly value "timing of brith" and to become as disciplined as possible in "birth control".

Like having 3 or 4 children within a short time frame, the parents must have available resources so that each child gets their individually needed care, attention, guidance, support, time and love. Now, ***this can easily be done*** if the parents were *intentional about their preparation*... meaning **pre-marital strategizing**. There is that word again, strategy. Making a plan of action in light of the principles and policies and promises of the people who will be raising those children. One of the biggest set back for entrepreneurs who have multiple business "ideas" is that when their first business hits a snag of some sort or becomes stagnant, they immediately believe it must be a sign to "give birth" and start their next business. What is the benefit for the entrepreneur if they begin to pursue the development of another business idea, even if that business has nothing to do with the present business that is ***bleeding***? Did all that make sense? Why would a entrepreneur start focusing on a new idea or business when the first one is not yet ***self sufficient*** or is presently in need of their undivided entrepreneurial focus? This dangerous shift happens when the entrepreneur begins to ***focus on revenue and income over the impact*** they said they desired to make when they first wrote their mission statement. Remember ...remember ... remember the mission.

- **This book is not about focusing on the income but the impact, knowing that if the impact is made the *needed* income will come.**

So here is the insight i provide my entrepreneurs with. How would you feel, if business #1 was able to help you launch business #2 ? How would it feel to be making the impact you want to make on the industry that you are in and your personal (essential) relationships not suffer, your quality of life not suffer, your finances not be stretched thin? Reminding them that **"success without compromise is possible"** is key for behavioral correction and perspective transformation. Unlike a parent who has two children back to back, the entrepreneur has the option to place his second business endeavor on the shelf or on the back burner in order to give business #1 what is needs to become self sufficient and then help them launch business #2. It's like parents waiting to have their second child until child #1 can walk, understand basic commands and is potty trained. Have you ever noticed how older siblings inherit the responsibility of baby sitting the younger siblings when the parents go out? It's like this with your business endeavors. If you ***strategize correctly***, we can set aside the needed resources and locate the best time to launch business #2 in such a way that business #1 could help raise business #2. So, again, how would you feel if business #1 was able to help you launch business #2?

The conversation of birth control is vital for every entrepreneur. It helps to prepare you on how to react and respond when business #1 is not producing the fruit, bringing in the cash or making the impact you expected it would "***by this time***". On the level of values and intentions ***every entrepreneur truly wants to give their best to everything they birth***. With the proper strategy every entrepreneur can do just that. But it requires that the "competitive mindset" be replaced with the "mission mindset". The danger with the competitive mindset is that too often the temptations that come with it will provoke you to *****birthing too soon**, spending too much and compromising your deepest morals simply **to say, "i came in first"**. Was that the mission? Was the initial aim *to come in first*?

- ***Entrepreneurs don't need competition, they need accountability.***

I know a lot of people want to come in first or be the best seller and i don't try to argue them down, i simply help them to remember their essentials and their overall mission so that they don't become distracted with a competition that yields no real reward nor an increase in profit… it simply strokes the ego. How valuable is "*that*" at the end of a quarter, what benefit does it bring your business? I remind my clients of their mission statement so that they take full advantage of the time they have been given to make the impact they have been *called to make.

So, how many children do you want to have? In the ability quadrant chapter, we took time to look at "resources". What relationships, material possessions, connections or money do you have in place that would help you start this business. Much of the idea behind birth control is having sufficient resources to raise the child. In many cases, people simply can't afford another child… unless they have help. The resources area of the quadrant truly helps us see the importance of having the right relationships in place to help us. I know you may have many business ideas you want to launch and birth...this means you are going to need to *increase your capacity*. One of the best ways to do that is to form **strategic partnerships**. In other words, sincerely connect with other business professionals and genuinely engage with them for the purpose of birthing a relationship *in which you help another through your specific area of gifting*. Imagine the entrepreneur who has 5 business ideas, but also multiple entrepreneurial friendships. Those relationships expand their capacity and makes it possible for those ideas to be birthed at a much higher rate of speed. Those relationships are sometimes like substitute teachers, they can step in and perform in times when the unexpected occurs ...and this is so valuable because it keeps the *flow of the business and helps *maintain the momentum* that is being built. It is like a married couple who has the support of both set of parents, other siblings and neighbors and has formed and maintained many community relationships. When they consider the idea of giving brith to another child, they have all these resources in their ability quadrant and that increases there capacity and confidence. So again, if you haven't read the Ability Quadrant chapter, i encourage you to do so. It will truly help you with brith control by helping you to answer the question, "am i ready to give birth?...and why?"

    Birth control is about the issue of *frequency*... and frequency, at it's core, is about timing and when it is all said and done, timing is a judgement call. The judgment that is being made is based on the desired outcome you have for your business. So, the more clear and detailed the desired outcome or the vision is, the better the "judgment call" can be.

To be able to birth a child or a business is a blessing. Don't let it become a ***burden***, simply because you didn't take time to consider the best possible time to launch.

SEVEN
WHAT IS YOUR STRATEGY?

I know what i want to do…
but *how* will i really get it done?

8-12 hours a day, 6 days a week, for 6 months …and no new clients, no new functional big ideas, no increase in revenue to afford to hire more help, no feeling of progress being made. How is that kind of return supposed to motivate anyone to keep trying and believing?

What does it really mean to "*try*"? Many people say that there is no trying, either you're doing it or you are not…simple. But is there more to trying than simply, "doing or not doing"? To try is defined as "***to attempt***",. So when people say, "i'm trying", do they really mean, I'm attempting, I'm putting forth the effort? In my experience–usually when an entrepreneur says i'm trying, what they are truly expressing is, "i have put forth effort but I'm not seeing the result i thought i would see by this time. Now although this is not the traditional definition of trying–this is the definition or underlined meaning that i've embraced for myself that explains the phrase "i'm trying". Has this ever been true for you?

Have you ever been asked, "how's it going?" And all you could do is put a semi-smile on your face and say with a tone of discontent, "i'm trying" …and then let out a huge sigh? How did you get to that place? What is it that the entrepreneur is missing, overlooking …or simply not doing that is causing them to "not see" the results they expected by this time?

- *Often this is because they are putting forth effort towards an "unclear vision" or "under detailed strategy".*

Now i will say this, "trying" is a great starting point. It is the base off of which a greater more effective effort can be built. I see "try" a lot like i see "faith". When people say "i tried", they are referring to past tense, an effort that is no longer in play–tried is what "they were doing" but have ceased to do. Imagine if i asked an entrepreneur , "do you believe you are going to succeed?", and they answered "i *believed* i was. The next question would most likely be, why did you stop believing.? This works the same way when i hear entrepreneurs tell me, "i tried"–i ask, "why did you stop trying?" Trying or **continuing to put forth effort is *the foundation on which ambition lives*.** Without your effort, what result can you expect. Again, referring back to faith; faith without works is dead. The moment you "stop believing" you will be successful is the moment in which being successful is no longer an option for you. **Your faith is *the foundation on which the *vision lives*.** So what makes an entrepreneur stop trying or stop believing? In many cases it is, *the return they see for the effort or sacrifice they put in.* It's 8-12 hours a day, 6 days a week, for 6 months ...and no new clients, no new functional big ideas, no increase in revenue to afford to hire more help, no feeling of progress being made. How is *that* kind of return supposed to motivate anyone to "continue trying and believing"? I am not writing this to pep talk you into trying again or to encourage you to "keep believing". No, my purpose for this chapter is to shed insight and hopefully add value to the importance of a ***strategy***.

- *"Potential is realized through the *discipline we put on the *details of the strategy".*

It is easier to "keep your commitments" when you put a clear detailed plan of action together to help you stay focused on the journey and stand firm in the process. If i could help you enhance or increase "***your return***" , continuing to put forth the effort wouldn't be a problem at all. But the return will not be enhanced or increased by just any actions or effort. It takes ***very specific actions that are tied into your present abilities and principles.*** It takes very specific actions that compliment your present opportunities and counter attack the present or potential threats. Success or progress doesn't come from just staying busy but from being productive. Strategy is not just doing anything , but it is doing specific things that are in alignment with the results of your "Abilities Quadrant" and the awareness of your purpose, identity and values. This may be a good time to go back and read chapter 1 because an effective strategy will always be based on the results of your "Ability Quadrant".

A plan, is a detailed *proposal*, but a strategy, is a plan of action or *policy* designed to achieve a major aim. Although they are very similar, in my coaching sessions i use the term strategy to emphasize we are not just discussing what you want to do. A plan is good but it is only part of the strategy. Imagine the strategy as a package or a box that is delivered to your door step. In that box you will definitely find a plan, but you will also find:

- the vision
- the mission statement
- core values
- the results from your abilities quadrant
- s.w.o.t. analysis
- industry research , stats and trends
- capacity calculator
- essentials vs pursuits list

Approaching your goal from this stance exponentially increases the chances of you obtaining your goal and **keeping your morals in tact** during the process. What i've found to be most effective at increasing and enhancing "*the results or return*" is to take very intentional time to look at the entrepreneurs personal principles, morals, life mission and promises that they have made to themselves. I do this because *if the "core essence" of the entrepreneur is not taken into consideration and set as the base on which everything else revolves*–we run the risk of losing or compromising a very essential and valuable portion of who they are.

If that happens, it directly affects the return or the "profit" that will be realized because a profit is what you've gained after you *****deduct** what you spent or lost to get it.

A policy is a course or ***principle*** of action. A principle is a ***fundamental truth*** that serves as the foundation for a system of belief or behavior or chain of reasoning. So, what are the fundamental truths for you? Do you have set boundaries or is your approach to do ***whatever it takes*** to get ahead in this industry? These questions are vital to the plan of action / strategy because they lay the foundation for the ***behavior*** and ***reasoning***. And the behavior and reasoning are two of the main components that greatly influence the "return and results" you see from the effort and hours you put in.

- *The Bible tells me, when i was a child, i thought as a child, i spoke as a child and i reasoned as a child, when i became a man, i put my childish ways behind me.*

Evolving from an employee mindset to the entrepreneur mindset will also require a shift in reasoning and "***this shift***" is usually birthed in the process of completing the ability quadrant. I usually ask my clients to make three promises to themselves concerning their business ventures.

1. i promise to always _____.
2. i promise to never . _____
3. i promise to remember _____.

It is in the answers they provide for questions like these, that we begin to put together a strategy that is specific to their abilities, identity and morals. The deeper we go into unpacking these answers, the stronger the foundation becomes. We are finding their "why".

- *Remember: "your why will only be as strong as the core value it is connected to."*

We are exposing the ***truest intention*** for their reason of existence. The more clear the driving force behind their ambition becomes, the more resilient they become. And when obstacles arise, motivation to "keep trying and keep believing" is no longer as issue because ***their behavior and reasoning is clearly, and consciously linked to the core of who they are*** and why they are in this business. When the entrepreneurs behavior and reasoning is *linked at such a deep level of their identity and purpose*–it reflects in all of their business choices. Business choices that originate from the core purpose and identity of the entrepreneur, breaks the blockage and enhances the return the entrepreneurs sees for the effort they have put in. This all happens because the effort is no longer just a suggestion, a proposal or a shot in the dark. Their effort is driven by their core values and precisely aimed at the initial mission of the business. This in essence, is how you bring the entire entrepreneurial endeavor into deeper alignment. When that happens, it increases and enhances their return because they are now operating their business with a *****new consciousness***. In short, the entrepreneur has found "their flow or their lane". Remember this from chapter 1:

- In the first lens we are **considering** the "natural gifting" a person has. What innate abilities do you possess? This question begins to set the stage for the revelation or deeper revelation of their "created purpose". Knowledge of created purpose is key to every entrepreneur because if what you are pursuing isn't tied into your purpose in anyway , the pursuit will most likely not provide you with any true *fulfillment, which for me is the "foundational condition" for success to be actualized. In the exploration of the entrepreneurs natural gifting we are finding not only their strengths but their advantage. A persons "natural gifting" are abilities given to them that are specific to their purpose. The natural gifting gives them an *advantage in a specific time, environment and industry to complete a specific mission.

The reason it is important for the entrepreneur to find their flow, their lane, be guided by their core principles and to allow congruency between their life consciousness and business consciousness is because *these elements support the reasoning behind you possessing the **divine gifting** in the first place.* You have been *****called** to this work and this industry and if you are not seeing the return or results you expected, you may begin to question if this is truly what you've been called to do. Strategizing in this way is one of the greatest defenses against doubt, stagnation and temptation. By now i hope that you see, in order to increase or enhance the return, you need a strategy because strategy is built on the awareness of your *divine* gifting and awareness of your "*divine* gifting" reminds you of your "*divine* advantage" to complete the assignment or accomplish the commission you have been sent to fulfill in *that* *specific industry. With this new consciousness as a foundation, you can begin to **better aim** your efforts so that you are not moving and reacting in desperation but rather in confidence because you have a clear vision and a <u>detailed strategy</u> that is consistent with your morals, compliments your personal life principles and has considered and is prepared for every obstacle because it has reduced every decision to a ***moral choice,*** knowing that if you have been called to this business and this industry, the main ingredient to increasing your return and success will be *staying true to who you have been called to be.*

Remember, once you know this is the industry you have been called to and gifted to impact, you now have the surety that; you belong there, you have what it takes and that it will be worth it. Your gift is the evidence that if you walk by faith and stay true to your morals, you will succeed.

- ***Your gift is the reason you will not have to compromise.***

I've learned that after "intentionally being" in a industry for a while and making any degree of impact, people will no longer see you …they will see what you stand for and life does the same. This is where your legacy begins to become etched in stone. The longer you stand on that stage and the longer you remain in that spotlight, people and life will begin to see deeper and deeper into "*your why*", your reason for existence. And it is in what they see in you in those highs and lows, those moments of *adversity and temptation* to compromise that will greatly influence how successful you will be at accomplishing your purpose in that industry, in that time, for those people. When we begin to understand success as being more than material possessions or monetary gain, we will begin to morally conduct ourselves in such a way that our hearts desires for our business *will begin to pursue us.* Yes, your hearts desires for your business will begin to pursue you because your purpose was clarified and your intentions purified. And when that shifts happens, return, increase, results, promotion, success, opportunity and expansion, will flow freely and will no longer be a problem…all because those things are no longer the aim. The strategy and the form, not just what you do, but "how you do" is now the aim and the focus. The return you want is a *byproduct of exercising a customized and that **evolved business practice** stands on principles like:

- *give and it will be given unto you and it is better to give than receive. No matter your industry, you are in the hospitality business and in the field of service, the focus is never the gain but the give.*
- *When "the give" is intentional , the return is inevitable.*

The specific "way" in which an entrepreneur *releases their specific gift* to a specific industry is what will open more windows of opportunity for the exchange of goods and services to take place. These are just a few of the things a "***true strategy***" provides. It begins with personal policy and journeys all the way through to your purpose and business practices. It all comes down to "your ***reason*** for existence" and "your ***reasoning*** when you face obstacles".

- *Your *reasoning relies on your reason and your reason relies on your vision and your vision relies on your strategy.*

EIGHT
HOW IMPORTANT IS KNOWING YOUR *NICHÉ*?

Do i choose my niche…or has my niche already chosen me?

Flow needs alignment. This means that all the moving parts of your business practices, business principles and business mission, need to compliment one another and operate in ***congruency***. More often than not, major blockage and the cause of stagnation is found in the "market **aim*" of the entrepreneur. The niche, if not understood and approached correctly can cause even the best idea to fall flat, even when the industry is in need of what it could offer. So, what is your niche? In the industry you have been called to, there is a plethora of likeminded, equally passionate, highly driven entrepreneurs. Imagine it as a community. A wide variety of entrepreneurs seeking this specific industry for a specific purpose. How do you know where you "fit in"? Do you go and set up your shop where there is the least amount of competition or where the most money can be made? How do you choose your role in this community?

The first way in which to best understand "a niche" is to understand that it is a *calling.

A calling is a strong urge toward a particular way of life… a vocation. A calling is "divine" in nature, it is a supernatural feeling of suitability for a particular people, place or thing. Understanding "a calling" is understanding that ***you have been drawn*** to this place, this industry, this cause, this mission by the creator of all things. This is a divine call that you are operating in. And "within that call" are very specific details, one being a specific "target market". The Call contains two parts, a where and a who. You know you have been called to your specific industry, now you have to look inside yourself, through the lens of your passion, gifts and your particular set of circumstances to discover the *who; which specific group of people, or specific area of problems, you have been called to within that industry. Considering your *niche is a powerful internal conversation to have because you are discovering the specific area of a industry in which there is the ***greatest demand for your specific set of skills and the gifting in which you express those skills through.*** You are discovering the place that is most suitable for you, not based on what you want to gain but what you want to deliver. Like a suit that you would wear for clothing, there is an area in your industry that has been *tailored specifically for you. Remember, you were built for this work and you've been called to this place and you can call this place… home. This is where you've been called to set up shop in this particular community of entrepreneurs. This is the role you have been called to play in the grand scheme of ***all that is at stake in this industry.***

- *When you have been called to a place and a people...understand that there is a *thirst for you there.*

There is a thirst for your gifting, abilities and passion. As we mentioned in previous chapters, there is a place reserved for you and there are specific people who have been praying and are remaining hopeful that you find your way to that place because they are the ones in need of the service or the product that you offer. And as powerful of a vision as this is, if you enter a industry seeking monetary gain instead of being "**niche intentional**", you will miss these people and the profit they bring. If hospitality and service are not on the forefront of your mind, you will *misplace yourself in that industry and miss the treasure that was reserved for you because the treasure is contingent on *that particular niche* being serviced by you with your gift.

Your niche is a specialized, profitable corner of a market, it is "the specific area" of a business, industry or endeavor in which your gifts give you the ability to be the most "profitable." Profitable meaning, where you can make the most significant impact and not lose yourself or neglect your essentials in the process. Answer this question. *What specific group of people in your industry are you most concerned for or most excited about impacting with your service or product?* The role you take in that community or industry needs to be directly influenced by the specific things you came to offer that industry. Who you target should be based on what you provide, not what you want to earn. You are in this industry to deliver a package, deliver a gift, a service, a product... and the names of the people in need have already been divinely placed on your gifting. It was always intended for you to touch and impact very specific people with the abilities that were given to you. When those specific encounters happens, when those specific people and families are affected by you intentionally walking in your gift and calling, you experience a level of fulfillment that can only be provided by a force beyond this world.

It's not hard to tell when you are walking in your purpose because there is a specific kind of joy and feeling of accomplishment that you get when you are on your path that you can't manufacture or find anywhere else. Understanding that *"fulfillment enters in through the niche"* – begins to help us see the true value of knowing our niche.

- *Since the niche is in the calling, the feeling of fulfillment and the realization of success can only be obtained by frequenting and having close contact with that specific target market.*

But don't be discouraged, a niche is not a limit, or a "only". It is a target market, but it is not the only area you can offer your service to. From the idea of "essentials vs pursuits", **servicing your niche as a priority** is a "*business essential*". As long as you are giving the needed effort and attention to your niche *first*, other business opportunities outside of your niche can be pursued without taking away from the core of why you have been called to this industry. It is in recognizing your niche and intentionally seeking to service the people you've been called to, that you can unblock the flow of profit or prosperity that is due to you. Prioritizing your niche means that you are in awareness of its value. You are aware that your niche was knitted into the fabric of your calling. There is an appointed place and a appointed time in which you have been called to reach specific people. If through, the abilities quadrant, you have discovered, "the exact time" for you to launch or expand your business, the next most important thing to discover is "the exact place and the people" to whom you have been called to.

To fully embrace the idea of a niche, you would need to deeply believe that all this stuff...your gifting, the circumstances that got you here, even you reading this book, were designed and set up by a very intentional God. To pursue a niche is evidence that you believe you have been called to this work and that there is something waiting for you here. A people, a treasure, a opportunity, a door way. Your niche is as specific as the trials that got you here today.

- *Each of the trials we face in life had the ability to develop a very specific gift inside of us in a very specific way, so that we could accomplish a very specific mission in that season.*

The trials or obstacles we encountered, *triggered something in us and that something it triggered wasn't random, it was very specific to our destiny...likewise our niche. Where we have been called to and the people we have been called to is not random, but specific to a need that is to be met. You were created and placed on this earth to "meet a need" and you have been given an entrepreneurs mind to meet that specific need in the specific industry that is in need of what you've been gifted with. So no, none of it is random. The moments when we think it is, it usually where we settled because we can't figure it out yet. So with the same intentionality that you were created with, i encourage you to move forward in your business endeavors.

- *Your niche will be discovered through the intentional exploration of the vision, your gifting, your passion and the specific set of circumstances that you grew up in or have been exposed to over time.*

It is vitally important to the *flow that you choose the niche that is most in alignment with the divine details of everything we have discussed so far in this book. **Stagnation thrives on dissonance**. "***Why you do***" and "***what you are***", are just as important as "***where you do it***" and "***whom you do it for***". I would encourage you to choose the right niche, but in all honesty, **you don't really choose your niche, your niche has really …already been chosen, it came with your calling.** So, if this is your time to launch or expand, i encourage you to move forward from here giving great consideration to the mission of your business and your desired legacy. If we take time to plan and strategize through pure intentions, we will see that it all lines up. From the moment God gave us the idea, to every moment in which we add value to someones life through that idea–has been divinely ordered. A calling is a pre-existing thing that you step into. It was prepared for you… **it is "your path"**.

NINE
3 THINGS YOUR CLIENT WANTS TO KNOW

Do you like them?
Can you help them?
Can they trust you?

When it comes to the core of our concerns, not much has changed since our childhood. The innate desires in our heart to be liked , to be helped & to be safe, still reigns supreme at our core. Did you know that your client was once a child ? Sounds like a silly question, but have you truly considered that *your clients were once "children" that experienced a "unique childhood" where they were exposed to an environment that "molded their understanding" and perception of life, relationships, humanity, justice and survival* ? The person on the other end of that phone , or looking you in the eyes from across that counter–they have endured so much life to bring them to this point, to your company, to your establishment, to your door step...now what ? Have you noticed that some of your clients come with a multitude of questions , others barely say a word, this has a lot to do with their childhood: **how they were raised and what they were exposed to.** Some demand a discount , some don't care what the rate is. Some are hesitant , some you have to slow down. Each client / customer is unique in many ways and has been "molded by life" into the person that you are interacting with. **Many times the entrepreneur can get lost and frustrated in the process of** trying to gauge the clients genuine interest. Sometimes the entrepreneur gets lost in trying to interpret the body language, attitude and the energy during their encounter with their customer. But how about i simplify that for you.

What if i could help you to enhance the encounters you have with your customers / clients in such a way that each interaction between the customer and your business resulted in "some sort of profit?" What if i could help you to enhance the encounters you have with your customers / clients in such a way that each interaction between the customer and your business resulted in:

- a deeper revelation of the value of your product or service
- a greater appreciation for your product or service
- and a greater trust for the person who is offering that product or service to them?

You want the customer / client to understand the value of your product / service. And if it fits their need, you want them to *i**nvest their time, treasure, energy*** into what it is you are offering. But did you know, at the core of it all, the customer has their own needs that they want you to see and appreciate, their own subconscious questions that they need answered before they can consider investing in your product or service. The customer desperately wants to know three very important things before they invest :

- Do you like me?
- Can you help me?
- Can i trust you?

These 3 questions should not only be the concern of the client– answering them for the client should be the main focus of the entrepreneur. These 3 questions were presented to me in a leadership summit and they stuck so deeply within me. I considered these questions for months and came to the conclusion that these are not new concerns. These are not workplace, service industry or business environment issues. These questions have been present *in all of us* long before we could properly express them in a complete sentence. Going back to our childhood, these questions were present. Before we knew what *****trust** was, we desired the feeling of *****safety**. Even before we knew what help was, we desired to feel *****supported**. Even before we really knew what it meant to like… or be like, we desired *****acceptance**. The customer, the client, the one you have been called to serve and provide a service to is primarily in need of these three essentials because they are the foundation of trust and without trust, how can you "properly service" those in need of what you are offering?

It reminds me of the "ice breaker activities" that many companies are now using prior to engaging employees or participants in workshops, trainings or meetings. The purpose of the *ice-breaker* is to break the ice… to warm the participants up so that they will open up and in turn allow the following information will be more easily absorbed. This is done by creating a welcoming and fun atmosphere where they engage in a person to person activity (that is usually un-related to the business at hand) so that they can get to **know and trust** the people they are about to engage with on a professional level. I believe these activities begin to **answer the core questions** of the participants and ease their reservations so that the will be willing to engage and invest in the opportunity at hand. I also believe these activities awaken the participants so that the true value of what is being offered will not be missed. The ice breakers *break down the walls* between everyone involved in the activity and *creates a bridge*. The "core questions"; do you like me, can you help me, can i trust you, are *the screening process filters* that we all use to protect ourselves from unwanted or potentially damaging encounters with other humans. Until those concerns are addressed and those questions answered by you the entrepreneur, you will remain outside, far removed from the client / customer and ineffective at whatever your endeavor is. Think about your last encounter with a client or customer. Do you think they felt accepted, felt supported, felt safe? Did they engage with you and behave in a way that made you believe they had opened up to you?

Did you initially and intentionally seek to interact with them to *purposefully gain their trust, show genuine interest in who they are as a person,* not just a client. Did you **listen** to understand their issue so that you could *clearly express your ability* to provide them with the needed service?

You have been called to this industry and to these people who truly thirst for what you have to offer, but none of that will amount to anything *unless you can build that bridge.* Until that wall is broken down, that bridge built, those core questions answered...you will remain outside of their castle, with your potential in hand, unable to make the impact you know that you've been called to make. Our gifts and our calling get us to the place and to the people, but here is where the tools and skills we have intentionally acquired play the biggest role in our effectiveness. To unblock the flow, the entrepreneur has to have more than an in-depth understanding of their industry and offer a quality product or service. The entrepreneur first must understand that **without the person to service, they don't have a business**. This should make understanding the *values of "the person" they call customer/ client the highest point of focus. Until they know that you genuinely care, until they know that you like them, can help them and they can trust *you*, they will continue to hold back or not invest, even if they know they need the product. The entrepreneur is the product, you are the service.

- *Before you offer a physical product or tangible service, you are offering yourself to the person.*

Take time to enhance that experience by seeking to address those core 3 questions every time you encounter them. This kind of "small talk" may seem pointless to some entrepreneurs , but **the value it adds to the person, customer, client, is huge**. *People **loyally go to where they feel the most valued**.* If you truly want to make a impact in your industry, seek to primarily *add value* to the people in that industry that need your specific service. This is how you release the flow and increase the profit, so that your intended purpose in that industry may be accomplished and realized.

TEN
THE CUSTOMERS IS *ALWAYS* RIGHT

**Is the customer always right
…even when they are wrong?**

The customer is always right… even when they are wrong? We think that the idea of the customer is always right is practiced by many companies to de-escalate situations in which the customer and the companies representative… disagree. If you've ever been involved in a disagreement with a customer or maybe you were the customer and you disagreed with the business practices of a company, you know that the situations can become very volatile and escalate very quickly. The conflict here usually arises when the customers expectations or desires are not taken serious, not sincerely considered or met with a reasonable response. In all honesty, in most cases, the representative that the customer is talking to has no "real power" to accommodate those desires or meet those expectations because they are company policy. One thing the representative does have power over, is "*how they interact*" with that patron during the conversation.

When it comes to **clients and conflicts**, what are you or your representative to do? Understand that every situation will require it's own unique approach but each approach should be rooted in this mindset; "the customer is always right". The phrase is simple but i feel it is often mis-understood at the foundation of its intended purpose. Pay close attention to this phrase, "the customer is always right and even though they are always right–they still may not get what they are verbally asking for".

- *The "customer is always right", is not about, changing policies or relinquishing control of your business over to the customer, rather it is intended to guide you into the most correct or most appropriate "**attitude** in which" to interact with a client or customer when there is a disagreement.*

For instance:

a customer is upset and complaining about a return or exchange policy. They feel they should have been given more time to return a product for a full cash refund. Now, your refund / exchange policy clearly states on the receipt and was verbally spoken to them by the cashier that the specific time frame in which they could make a return or exchange and the conditions therein. But now they are back at the store, wanting special privileges that go against the expressed pre-set policy that was put into place by the powers that be.

In situations like these it's common for the customer to want to speak to a supervisor or a "higher up", someone with more *power and influence. What they want is to speak to someone who can accommodate their desires, even if it's against the policy. So, what do you do? Shift your mindset. Remember the previous chapter: do you like me, can you help me, can i trust you. As an entrepreneur *these three questions are what drive the intention in which we interact with our customer / clients.* When a customer or client encounters you or someone you have hired or partnered with, they are encountering the **mission**, **intention** and the **heart** of your business. The values of your business should clearly be expressed in **how* you and your partners interact with the most valuable asset to your business...the client.

So, how do we approach this idea that "the customer is always right" when the customer is clearly "*wrong?" Hear them out. Acknowledge their desire and express no **personal** counter argument against how they feel. Remember , the customer feels like it should be different and their feelings are not incorrect. In these situations, **conversations become conflicts when:**

1: the customer feels they are not being heard.
2: the customers feelings are not being taken into consideration.

The **validity* of the core emotional response of the customer are not to be argued. The objective in this situation for anyone interacting with a customer / client, is to C.A.R.E: **consider, acknowledge, respect, extend.**

C   consider their position , perspective

A   acknowledge their feelings

R   show them the utmost respect

E   extend the most reasonable and legal compromise

We do this in order to help **preserve the relationship** and in turn enhance the possibility of a later exchange of investment or a referral. Even if policy doesn't allow you to give them what they are asking for, there is no need to burn that bridge. You can still provide a service to them by "helping" redirect them to another company where their specific needs can be met. To have a genuine concern for your customer and client is the main focus here but this is hard to do if you are not consistently putting yourself in remembrance of their value and your calling to serve them. It's easy to be friendly, supportive and attentive when the customer comes and makes their purchase but the "evolving entrepreneur" must understand that it is also good business practice to greet them with *that same attitude* when they come back for the exchange, or have an issue with the policy.

- This can be a emotional topic for many entrepreneurs so let me be clear. You have not been called to be a push-over. There are some customers who simply refused to be pleased and bring their emotional baggage to your establishment… but recognizing, "no matter your business–you are always in the service industry", reminds you that you are "***here to help***". Don't allow yourself to get bent out of shape. Nothing is being threatened, it is only a disagreement. The bible says, "**how can two walk together if they don't agree**". In these disagreements remember this verse and understand that maybe this customer / client is no longer meant to ***walk with you***. Even if this is the case, you still want to help them along their way. You still want the conclusion of this business relationship to end on a positive helpful note. With all the sincerity inside of you, simply redirect them to another company where their specific needs could be better accommodated. This mode of conduct is how you keep from "losing your passion" for the industry that you love. This prevents you from becoming tainted or jaded. One very important thing i've learned in business is, "everyone that comes, isn't meant to stay". Although customer loyalty is very important, company morale trumps it, every time. It takes us back to the **essentials vs pursuits** conversation we had in the previous chapters. The customer or customer loyalty is the pursuit, but if the relationship with that customer is ***proven to be poisonous to the morale and mission*** of the company, that customer must go. ***Whenever an essential is threatened, a serious and immediate response must be made to preserve the essence of what keep your organization moving forward***. Protecting the heart of your business is always essential # 1. Ok, so i'm happy we had that little discussion, let's move on.

"The customer is always right", is not about policy, *but about attitude.* What i want to be clear about here is that the attitude that the customer is met with greatly influences the profit you will experience. This is because–every person that you encounter on a business level instantly becomes advertisement. Wether that advertisement is good or bad is dependent on the energy and spirit you present in that encounter. It is not dependent on if the person acquired the service or product they wanted, it is dependent on **how* they were serviced. or **how well** they were served. Wether they leave with the product or not, they have become a walking business card. Companies spend a lot of money on marketing and advertisement and this approach to "customer service" really reduces that cost because it **maximizes** the free opportunity to make a positive impact on the very people the company would later try to reach through advertisement. The people you encounter on a business level will always go and tell at least one person about their experience and that person will most likely tell someone else also and so on. Now that you've gained a deeper understanding of the exponential value that one encounter with one person can truly have on your business, what adjustments are you looking to make in **how you respond** to emails, voice messages, customer feedback? In what areas of customer / client interaction can you be more intentional?

- *If the person didn't like your product or your policy, but loved your service, that person can still be the source of a referral.*

Never underestimate the value of good customer service. How you treat the customers that have been entrusted to you will greatly influence the flow and profit that you are allowed to experience. Remember that this is a *calling. You have been called to this industry and to these people and with that comes a great responsibility to add value wherever possible.

- *The pre-meditated assault on stagnation isn't rooted in directly trying to increase the profit, but in executing in alignment and at a higher level of excellence. This enhances *how efficiently and effectively we service the people we are privilege to serve*.

As simple as it sounds, "service with a smile" will always be one of the most powerful ways to create an environment for expansion, longevity and prosperity.

CELEBRATE *OFTEN*

Appreciation fuels discipline and determination

"A person who feels appreciated will always do more than is expected". And what better way to show appreciation than through celebration. Publicly acknowledging someone in a social gathering or a fun activity could be the boost your company needs to break the stagnation. Celebrating the seemingly small victories, is key to maintaining the morale of the office and the motivation for all who work with you, and for you.

- *I am a firm believer that frustration is a result of unmet expectations and i believe that subconsciously every human being expects some sort of acknowledgement for their participation, especially in a business endeavor.*

And honestly, shouldn't they receive that public acknowledgement for their participation on top of their weekly or monthly pay check?

When we take a moment to consider what it really takes to make a business "run smoothly and profitably", there are many components that must be in sync and that doesn't happen without real person-power and man-hours. Consider the real discipline and the real sacrifice that real humans are making for the mission of your business to be accomplished. It is from this place of awareness that i help my entrepreneurs *infuse a consistent regimen of celebratory activities* ,to remind, not only their employees, but the family and friends of the employees that they, the boss, is aware of what it takes and is grateful for all those who sacrificed in order to help make the dream a reality. Again, those who feel appreciated will always do more than is expected. *A paycheck covers the legal reimbursement for the expressed duties but *appreciation is the catalyst for the "over and above work ethic" that almost every employer truly desires their employees and volunteers to operate in.*

Rather you have one volunteer, one intern, one employee or a team of 30 people working for you, the continued flow of your business is greatly influenced by the mental and emotional well-being of those turning the wheels. *Expressed appreciation greatly enhances both the mental and emotional state of the person being appreciated.*

- *What type of profit or impact do you think you would make if those who worked for you not only believed in the vision but performed the duties with a passion very similar to your own?*

The key here for the entrepreneur is not to try and butter up those who work for you or try and buy them off with gifts and prizes. The key insight here is that *"whatever you acquire requires maintenance."* If you are fortunate enough to acquire "help" in the form of volunteerism or employment , recognizing what it will take to help that person realize their fullest potential in your company is vital to the continued growth of your company. Realizing *the part you play* in helping the potential of that person to be realized is an even bigger part of the puzzle that i help my entrepreneurial clients put in place in the "strategy phase".

- *If a person lacks *passion, *focus or *appreciation–it will show in the quality of their service and their work ethic.*

Honestly, discipline results more from "presently feeling appreciated" than it does from their emotional or mental connection to the future reward. For a person to stay motivated and actually build momentum, the reward can not always be far off in the future. Attainable present day goals and scheduled celebratory activities on the weekly or monthly calendar to reward those goals being met–are what truly helps the company to build momentum. When the employer is intentional about "adding value" to the lives of those who are turning the wheels and helping make the dream a reality – **the business becomes "blessed" because the culture of the business is "to be a blessing"**. This is the shift that "celebrations" cause. It moves the consciousness and culture of the company from a "***taking for granted***" behavior pattern–to a "***taking a moment***" to consider the value of all those actively participating in the success of this companies mission. Again, when done correctly, this is not limited to just the employees but to the family and close friends of the employees because they are the "essentials" of the employee. *(to better understand *essentials visit the chapter entitled "essentials vs. pursuits).*

In order for appreciation on that level to be shown the employer must allow themselves to become more *present during their interactions with their employees and volunteers so that the *values of the employees and volunteers can be recognized during the encounters they have with them.

- *Knowing what a person *values is the key component when intentionally aiming to help them feel appreciated by the celebration.*

Knowing things like their favorite snack or meal, their personal pursuits, anniversaries or familial milestones, will help you aim your celebratory efforts in such a way that the employee not only feels appreciated but they feel valued and supported… is that the kind of person you would like to be remembered for being?

In closing this chapter, i wanted to make sure that i didn't miss the main goal, which is to remind the entrepreneur to ***celebrate themselves**. Even "you" will do more than is expected of yourself when you publicly show yourself appreciation* or allow others to show you appreciation for the steps you are taking toward making the impact you set out to make. For the select group of entrepreneurs i've worked with, "receiving" seems to be a serious struggle. Celebrating themselves or letting others celebrate them seems to always be a at the "bottom of the list", …if it's on the list at all. Today i'd love for you to understand that the principle remains to be true *even when it comes to celebrating you. Those who feel appreciated will always do more than is expected.* It will enhance your discipline, the quality of your work, your work ethic, your desire to go over and above, your peace and the level of fulfillment you experience along this entrepreneurial journey. You can't pour from an empty vessel and appreciation is one of the ways to keep "what's in you" pouring out smoothly to those around you. When speaking to those who have sold their company, retired or passed their business on to a family member or friend, the conversations seems to always visit this point; "*i wish i had enjoyed it more or started enjoying it sooner*".

You should enjoy what you have been called to do, i believe it should be a requirement because i see it as a vital business practice for the sake of the morale of the office and the legacy of the company. For all those who come into contact with what you have created through your company… may they be forever changed and *personally enhanced* due to the celebratory practices, that you made non-negotiable, while leading your team to quarterly victories and yearly profits.

TWELVE
REST & MEDIATION

Why do i rest …but don't feel rested

Here we are, the final chapter and surprisingly the most difficult chapter for me to write. Difficult because of the "***drift***" i allowed to happen. Let me explain. I had a "due date" by when i wanted this book to be done and sent off to my publisher… and I'm presently in those final hours. Like many entrepreneurs, i began to be ***blinded by my own ambition.*** If not properly partnered and kept in check with a strategy, founded on core values and principles, ambition alone will cast a very dark and deep shadow over your *essentials, safety and the importance of "the spirit of excellence" in which you have been called to perform.

I was so close to the finish line that all i began too focus on ***was*** the finish line. It all became a race against time and i began to "break form", not focusing on my breathing. I began to stop doing all the essential things that i just finished writing about in this book. Those same essential things that got me this close to the finish line. How did this happen …why did i "drift?" I did what i've seen so many entrepreneurs do as a precursor to their downfall. I began subconsciously running from something that wasn't even chasing me. That was, the ***Failure of not finishing***. I remind myself often of the importance of *finishing what i start. For whatever reason, fear crept in as i approached the completion of this literary project.

- *I was ahead of schedule and i began to pride myself on my progress *alone but that caused me to loosen my embrace of the process.*

Embracing the process is what keeps the entrepreneur committed to the detailed step-by-step investment they must make in order to experience completion…but i had *drifted. Having a great inner circle of accountability partners is what brought this to my attention. I was asked, "Donovan, what is this last chapter that you're struggling to write?" I replied, "the importance of rest."…and boom, there it was! That is exactly what i needed. Had i been neglecting my rest? Had i been so focused on teaching it, that i neglected to practice it? Why did i begin to struggle so much with the thought of not completing this project? How did i drift? I honestly began to become anxious and that began to "fog my thoughts". Imaginations of me not completing this book, drove out *"the vision of completion"* that i had previously held as the screen saver in the forefront of my mind. How could i neglect to protect that "vision"? I drifted. I knew i had been called to this and i knew i had what it took, so what was the problem? This onset of fog, confusion, writers block, had crept in through an open door. A door that many entrepreneurs miss when doing their daily checklist ...*meditation*.

- ***Although many entrepreneurs struggle with "taking a load off" and resting, they all eventually take some down time. Either voluntarily or as a result of "vehicle breakdown."***

To rest is to "cease from work" or movement in order to relax, refresh or to recover your strength. Understand this, just because you "take a load off" doesn't mean you will experience relief, renewing or recovery. We know we need to "*take a load off*"...but what do we need to "*put back on*" in order to experience true relief, reassurance, relaxation, or a release from anxiety? If we don't learn how to truly take this "temporary break"... we will become broken.

Look at it this way: **Rest** *is the stage that we set in order to recover*. Rest is not the completion of what should be done, *it is only the beginning.* Rest is the stage ...and meditation is what we are to do on that stage. I am not going to lock you into a specific definition or *way* of meditating but i do want to invite you to have this conversation with yourself.

- *What is it that i need to do—while away from work, in order to experience relief, renewing and recovery ?*

This question is paramount because no matter how much potential a entrepreneur may have, **if they can't access that potential, they will

not operate in their greatest self. If the entrepreneur is not truly "themself", how do you think that affects their ability to organize and manage their business ? The effectiveness of the entrepreneur is primarily determined by the sharpness of the tool and the health of the vehicle in which they "***entrepreneur through***", which is a sharp mind and a healthy body. Those are the exact essentials that "rest and meditation" help you to maintain. You simply aren't quite your "best" self when you don't take care of yourself physically, mentally, emotionally and spiritually. I must express how vital these last two chapters are to the "**evolution of the entrepreneur.**" Celebration, rest and meditation are irreplaceable essentials in the entrepreneurs pursuit of success.

I drifted because i took the time, i set the stage, but i stopped meditating. I took time to rest, but my thoughts were of the finish line alone. No matter how motivating it may have been at times to see the finish line being so close, it didn't relieve me, renew me or help me to recover. Like a boxer between rounds:

- I went to my corner but i didn't sit down and rest my legs. I didn't drink water and hydrate my body. I looked across the ring at my opponent but i didn't listen to my coaches (mentors) corrections and instructions. I had a break from fighting, so in a way i "took a load off" but i didn't intentionally "put anything on" that would give me an advantage once the fight resumed.

Likewise for the entrepreneur, i encourage the *****intentional rest*** and the prepared mediation. *Taking your mind off the pursuit,* off the endeavor, off the project, is not a weakness and it won't kill you. But to the polar opposite extreme, ***it will make room for your strength*** to rise up and excite new life for the remainder of the journey.

So, how did i correct my drift ? First, i considered how much of this book i had written and i realized that by now in chapter twelve i may need *more rest between chapters* than i previously did. So, believe it or not, i *took *more* intentional time away from this project. So close to the finish line, but by the help of my accountability partners i realized that at this point, **my *need* for my essentials had increased** The second thing i did was *look to my* "essentials list" that i have written on my white board. ***I began to take that intentional time away from this project,*** to do more of the things on my essentials list. Remember, your pursuits are, what you are after, your essentials are, what you are made of. Sample essentials are: time with family, your favorite beach, favorite meal or going to the gym.

Your essentials are what make you tick. Being led by ambition alone can cause the entrepreneur to forget the importance of "***prioritizing the essentials and balancing the pursuits***" and that is a recipe for stagnation, frustration and entrepreneurial sabotage. The third thing i did was **revisit my vision**. There is a joy that comes with imagining the manifestation of what once seemed to be unimaginable. I opened my folder and visited the vision i have written out for my ***life legacy***, my ***career*** and my soon to be ***marriage***. I didn't just read it, i activated my imagination and i saw myself in it. I immersed myself into the vision through all five of my senses. I considered not only what it would look like, but what it would smell like , sound like, taste like and feel like. What a beautiful and inspiring experience that was. Considering my present capacity, understanding my present needs, diving into my essentials and awakening my senses to the forthcoming manifestations–truly gave me great relief. I felt thoroughly renewed but there was still one more thing i needed to do. I needed to ***re-cover***, return to a normal state of health, mind and strength. In my meditation time i needed to **re-cover** or *"go over" very specific parts of my strategy.* I **verbally** reminded myself, sometimes through chanting, of:

- who iAm
- what I've been called to do
- why i will succeed at it.

Recovery is experienced at it's best when the entrepreneur takes time to go over and re-visit their 3 promises and their Ability Quadrant. Doing these things were the catalyst for my recovery because they all reminded me that *"i was covered"*. They reminded me that iAm anointed and called for the work that i had set out to do. This is the power of rest and meditation. Why step away from the work if you are only going to come back *feeling* the same way you did when you left? How can someone close their eyes for 6-8 hours every night but still wake up tired? They *set the stage* but didn't do anything profitable with it. Consider these :

- the last thing we do before bed.
- the music we listen to while sleeping.
- the images in our mind before we doze off.

We have all these amazing opportunities to be more intentional with our "away time" and to experience true relief, renewing and recovery every night. How much more enhancement could we experience when we take an intentional day or two to rest and meditate? Nothing resets my energy and renews my strength more than remembering that i have been divinely anointed for this work and appointed to this time and that *it will be worth the effort that i'm required to invest*.

- *Take on the meditation. Form the habit and then allow the habit to form you.*

My hope for this chapter is that you resist allowing your ambition to fool you into over-extending yourself and overcommitting your schedule. Remember the power of the essentials and the life that they bring. This chapter on rest and meditation, coupled with the chapter on celebration, are intended to help you to recognize the two major essentials of every entrepreneur. It is from "the appreciation we experience" from being **publicly acknowledged** and "the recovery" we experience from *intentional rest and meditation*–that we are **enabled and empowered** to accomplish and *exceed our entrepreneurial goals. Celebration, rest and meditation are investments *in self* and without them the journey simply isn't quite as enjoyable, fulfilling or rewarding. So celebrate your progress, take a load off and ***put "life" on***.

This is the Entrepreneurs code :

To keep the mind sharp and the body healthy, for without these being maintained there is nothing more that the entrepreneur can expect to gain. But if you take care of the vehicle that you have been given to "entrepreneur through", there is nothing as an entrepreneur that you will not be able to do.

-DonovanDeeDonnell

MY CONCLUSION :

Were you changed or challenged? Did you experience true moments of revelation? What impacted you the most ...and what are you going to do about it? My prayer is that the seeds i planted took root. That they were digested, you were enhanced and that your entrepreneurial life will never be the same.

By now I'm sure you agree that this book is not a one time read. The "consciousness chapters" are your foundation. They are there for you when you begin to question,

- Why do i do this ?
- Do i have what it takes ?
- Have i been called to this work ?
- and similar questions like these.

Understand that these questions will show up from time to time, attached to very strong emotions. It is very normal but remember that emotions are not our guide. Refer back to these chapters and your own personal side notes when situations like these arise.

The "commitment chapters" are your *footing*. They are there to keep you on your path and "in-step" with the ***divine timing*** of your life. When you begin to wonder;

- Is now the time ?
- Is this the way ?

Refer back to these chapters for clarity. Many cross-roads will present themselves along your path but remember that this book has already helped you to set ****pre-determined* responses** to situations like these.

The "care chapters" are your covering. They work as the premier ***preservers*** of your entrepreneurial flow, your inner peace and your inner alignment. Without the insight obtained in these chapters, success, fulfillment, peace and profit will be short lived.

If you've realized through your journey of this book, that you have definitely been called to entrepreneurship, understand; ***that does not mean you've been called to become consumed by it.*** Don't let your passion become your frustration. When there is limited to no flow, remember that you have ***12 chapters of ammunition***, specifically designed for the War on Stagnation… all you must do is load your weapon and attack.

Being an entrepreneur could be risky but a good entrepreneur is taught to properly calculate those potential risks in hopes to avoid failure and loss. But don't misunderstand, even with the best calculations, exposure to danger is inevitable. So in order for an entrepreneur to respond to that inevitable danger in such an unstable and unpredictable environment and still make a consistent profit, they must begin to focus on the only environment that they truly have significant control over ... their own **consciousness**. The entrepreneur must remember to "stay present". It is from that awakened state that the evolved entrepreneur is enabled to operate, create and flow, in their industry, unrestrained. When an entrepreneur has a perspective shift like this , it causes the entrepreneur to realize that ***inner purification and alignment*** is the corner stone on which a truly successful business builds it's legacy. An entrepreneur that desires to see real profit, must calculate, not only the risk that comes with entering this unpredictable industry but also the risk that comes with not prioritizing "inner alignment" prior to entering that industry.

The "entrepreneurial experience" we have, while organizing and managing our business, is always a reflection of our truest intentions and our core alignment. Understand this: ***the War is won from within and the flow is released from within because at *conception, every bit of potential that you needed to win ...was already living within you.*** iPray that this book helps you tap into and gain access to the beautiful greatness that was divinely placed in you by God your creator. Know what you possess, know who needs it and know when's the best time to release it! Stay committed to this evolution process. We are not seeking to survive, we are seeking to thrive but that only happens when we become the threat.

"To see your business become all it could be, you can't simply seek to navigate the waters, you must learn how to create the weather. If you want to obtain flow, you must first create... alignment."

-DonovanDeeDonnell

My Conclusion :

- *your keep*SAKES :

on these pages

write down the most impactful quotes, phrases

or ideas that stuck out to you.

(*a few have been provided for you*)

"A test ...is evidence that you are being considered for a promotion"

"Potential is realized through the *discipline we put on the

*details of the strategy".

Remember, people don't always plan to compromise,

they simply fail to identify their *non-negotiables.

My Conclusion :

- myMeditation :

my.MANTRA●

this is the day that the Lord has made
i will rejoice and be glad in it
the favor of God is all over my life
and the joy of the lord is my strength
and the same God who takes care of me
will provide all my needs according to His riches in heaven
no weapon formed against me shall prosper
because all things are working together for my good
i am healed , healthy , blessed and prosperous
i am like a tree planted by the rivers water
and whatever i touch will prosper
i am the head
and not the tail
above and not beneath
the lender and not the borrower
and joyfully i give to those in need
and never will i lack
i am forgiven
i am soon to be happily married
i am energy wrapped in flesh
thank you father God for enlarging my territory
so that i may more perfectly honor you with my gift
thank you for partnering with me
so that i may properly steward this blessing
and thank you for leading me not into temptation
so that i will not mess it up.

(biblical scripture inspired)

- myJourney :

I thought it would be a beautiful thing to invite you into a more in-depth look into how i got to where iAm today. For the most part i've been self-employed or an independent contractor since 1999 and that is not an easy feat in the city of Los Angeles. I've been in the trenches, i've experienced the plenty and i've endured the famines. From personal fitness training, to real estate, to selling life insurance, to public motivational speaking, to life coaching and much more, i've seen what works and what doesn't work in the world of entrepreneurship. I was taught at a young age to stay present and aware. I was taught to be intentional about observing the *inner workings* of the environments i was planted in. That training allowed me to see with great clarity that success and failure were not random. The benefit of studying the "*lineage of success and failure*" is that you can trace success and failure back to the "location of conception". It is the *mindset*, the *core values* and the *intentions* of the entrepreneur that have proven to be the "breeding ground" that gives way to either success or failure. This is where i began to understand the true value of purification and alignment in the life of the entrepreneur.

One of the greatest components of my professional career, that awakened me to the foundational psychology of entrepreneurship, was the time i invested going through the "Awyken Professional Life Coach Training" Course, where i graduated in 2014. Since then i have intentionally pressed my way to further my understanding of Neurolinguistics

Programming, Psychology, Sociology and *Energies. It was (and still is) through my private studies, leadership seminars and personal mentor trainings that i found (and continue to find) depth to my understanding and the tools needed to support the evolution of my gifting. My love for seeing people embrace their true self and live a life of purpose and fulfillment has been the driving forces behind the books i have written. I've jumped into the industry of entrepreneurial development with both feet because i know it is where i belong and like you, the places we have been called to is where we will make the greatest impact and experience the most success.

I have spoken and hosted trainings in the fields of *leadership, entrepreneurship, personal development, pre-marital preparation, depression and suicide prevention* in multiple cities in California and Texas and abroad in Brazil and South Africa. This industry has a deep and unique thirst for the *gift* i have come to offer and the personality through which i serve it. It is from my own experience, research and training that i write this book and it is my {*divine gifting*} in this specific field that has granted me *privileged access* to you... the amazing person reading this sentence. Your presence and purpose on this earth are important to God your creator and i am here to help you see entrepreneurship in a entirely new light, so that you may experience growth, expansion and success in a variety of new and beautiful ways. *"Helping you see, is important to me but helping you evolve is vital for all".*

You are not here by accident, this is divine appointment.
May your eyes be opened and mind forever awakened.
iAm DonovanDeeDonnell and
iAm here to *change the way you think.*

*

DonovanDeeDonnell.com

Thank you for Everything

CPSIA information can be obtained
at www.ICGtesting.com
Printed in the USA
FFOW03n1630120717
37694FF

9 781545 604113